CREATING THE LOOK

Swedish Style

Katrin Cargill

CREATING THE LOOK

Swedish Style

Photographs by Christopher Drake

Pantheon Books, New York

For David, with love, always.
With very special thanks to Anna Lallerstedt Thomas.

Copyright © 1996 Frances Lincoln Limited
Text copyright © 1996 Katrin Cargill
Photographs by Christopher Drake, copyright © 1996 Frances Lincoln Limited
Photograph on pages 18-19 copyright © Ingalill Snitt
Artwork on pages 76-7 copyright © 1996 Susanne Haines
Artwork on pages 121 and 131 by Amanda Patton copyright © 1996 Frances Lincoln Limited

Library of Congress Cataloging-in-Publication Data
Cargill, Katrin
Creating the look: Swedish style/ Katrin Cargill.
p. cm.
ISBN: 0-679-75891-7 (pbk.)
1. House furnishings – Sweden. 2. Interior decoration – Sweden.
I. Title
TX311.C37 1996
645'.09485 – dc20
96-13425 CIP

Printed in Hong Kong
First American Edition
1 3 5 7 9 8 6 4 2

Contents

Foreword

The unpretentious charm that pervades the town houses and painted farmsteads of Sweden is one that many visitors long to take home. Exterior walls are limewashed in glowing ochres and pinks, while bright Falun red adorns the timber buildings of the countryside. Inside their houses, Swedish people preserve their traditional past not only through their family celebrations at Christmas and Midsummer but in the lightness and elegance of their interiors. Over the last hundred years Swedish style has travelled around the world. During the lean years in Europe at the turn of the twentieth century, migrants from Scandinavia took it to the United States. There it can still be seen in the country homes of Connecticut. In Germany and Central Europe, many people discovered Swedish interiors through the paintings of Carl Larsson and were inspired to throw off the sombre clutter of the previous century.

Now the pared down lines and natural materials of Swedish style are proving equally attractive to today's designers and homeowners. And because it is so unpretentious, even the most timid decorator can achieve a similar effect. There is no need for structural alterations. Drape a plain muslin swag at the window. Put a coat of paint on a shabby old piece of furniture. For skirtings, doors and window frames use the distinctive pale grey that has come to be associated with the Swedish look. In many cases, it may be a question of reducing rather than adding to a room. Choose furniture and accessories that are simple but functional and that create an impact, then position everything carefully so that each piece can be appreciated separately and as part of the whole picture.

This book is intended to inspire and guide everyone who is looking to bring a little tranquillity into their home. As the perfect antidote to the stress of modern life, Swedish style will surely continue to be popular for many years to come.

Katrin Cargill

The Essence of Swedish Style

Traditional Swedish style is composed of many elements, both witty and practical. Whimsical marbling appears on walls and furniture in a country farmhouse; simple woven loose covers in cotton or linen protect upholstered seats beneath; a neat checked ribbon holds a picture on the wall. There is an emphasis, too, on the kind of composed calm that can be achieved very easily by arranging a pair of simple chairs symmetrically on either side of a chest of drawers or a drop-leafed side table.

The importance of light and sunshine to a nation that has always lived and worked through long dark hours in the winter is abundantly evident. Walls are generally painted in pastel shades, but may also be brightened with spattering, stencilling and other paint effects in vibrant colours. Windows are left completely bare or shaded only by plain blinds and curtains made of muslin or cotton, so that maximum use can be made of natural light. Double- or triple-glazing means that heavy drapes are not needed to keep out the cold in winter. As the days grow shorter, Swedes like to enhance the effect of artificial lighting with the warm glow of candles set in a window, placed on a table or reflected in a mirror so their light is doubled.

Considerable thought is given to the placing of furniture, not only for aesthetic reasons but also to ensure that, when sitting, people retain a sense of contact with the world outside or with the next room. Even if home is an apartment in the city, curtains and doors are not closed at any time of year, while in summer, windows are left open too.

Wood is another feature that is crucial to Swedish style. Fifty-eight per cent of the country is forested, largely with softwoods such as Scots pine and Norway spruce. Virtually all furniture is made of these simple woods, so over the centuries the Swedes have developed a talent for painting it to make it appear sophisticated and refined. Softwoods have also been used for floors, in place of marble or stone which had, for the most part, to be imported. Wooden floors were either scrubbed and left bare, covered in white or silver-grey paint to reflect the light, or, in grander homes, painted to mimic more expensive woods or parquet.

In homes where the basic furnishings were kept deliberately plain, accessories were selected for their elegance or for the craft skills which had gone into their creation, as well as for their practical uses. Delicate chandeliers and sconces held the ubiquitous candles. Fine porcelain in pale colours, crystal drinking glasses and monogrammed damask adorned the dining tables of the wealthy, while country women used unbleached linen as a basis for drawn-threadwork and cross-stitch hangings to decorate both bedrooms and living areas. Rag rugs made from old clothes added a splash of colour to wooden floors.

Today, as interest in the design of the past is flourishing, the techniques used to create traditional Swedish style are being adopted again. Reproduction furniture is now so beautifully made by Swedish craftspeople that much of it is superior to contemporary pieces. Whereas a couple of generations ago an antique chair might have been smartened by the addition of yet another coat of paint, now those same layers of paint are being removed and the original condition of the piece restored with the help of authentic materials and skills. The soft finishes achieved by water-based distempers and limewashes are rediscovering their previous popularity as subtle backgrounds to painted friezes and borders, *trompe-l'oeil* moulding and imitation stone effects.

This four-sectioned window in a seventeenth-century hunting lodge is hung with what has come to be a trademark of the Swedish style: a draped muslin swag tied with simple rosettes at the corners. On the walls there are well-preserved canvas panels, painted with a charming floral border in pinks and reds. The gilded Rococo mirror hung between two windows reflects light from the other side of the room. There is a spare softness to the elegance of this room, an effect enhanced by the use of pale greeny-grey paint for the woodwork rather than the harsh brilliant white more common in British or American interiors. Pots of red pelargoniums are often placed on window sills, where they thrive throughout the summer.

LEFT *This seventeenth-century wing of a former hunting lodge is painted in the yellow and white generally reserved for stone manor houses and noble residences, though by the mid eighteenth century this colour scheme had also begun to appear on wooden houses. Wings were usually detached buildings placed on either side of the main house, which contained the formal* salle *for entertaining. Typically one was used as a kitchen while the other was for guests.*

RIGHT *In the entrance hall to the main house, walls made of rough planks are painted with simple garlanded panels. The enfilade effect, in which several rooms are seen at once, is a common feature in Swedish homes. It allows the maximum amount of light to filter into each room and gives vistas from one end of the house to the other. Here the view is from the hall through the pale blue kitchen to the garden on the other side. The formality of the room layout makes a lovely contrast with the naïve wall decoration and bare floorboards.*

Having been a largely agrarian people for so many centuries – a hundred years ago over 90 per cent of the population still lived on the land – it is not surprising that many Swedish town dwellers today aspire to a second home in the country. Some families have owned summer houses for generations, and over the past twenty or thirty years there has been a renewed interest in restoring country cottages or *stugor*, which are usually of timber construction.

Indeed, the majority of Swedish houses are based either on the sixteenth-century *parstuga* or on the six-room ground plan of late seventeenth-century homes. The *parstuga* (literally 'double cottage') consisted of two separate sections linked by one room, often the entrance hall, which divided family living rooms from those used for special occasions. In the grander,

six-roomed house, the most important room was the central *salle*, which was kept for entertaining and generally stood between the two suites belonging to the lord and lady of the manor. To protect these from the dangers of fire, the kitchens were sometimes sited in another building.

Whatever the size and scale of the home, however, an emphasis was placed on visual links between rooms. Interconnecting doors would generally be left open, anticipating modern open-plan living, so that the eye was carried across the hall from one side of the house to the other. As the *salle* evolved into a general reception room or *salon* by the end of the eighteenth century, the main rooms continued to be built in an enfilade of communicating spaces looking out over the gardens.

Baroque to Rococo

Although modern Swedish style has been shaped by many European trends over the centuries, every fresh influence has been adapted to suit the country's limited natural resources. Inevitably, fluctuations in national wealth have also left their mark. Simplicity resulted as much from poverty as from aesthetics. People used the only materials they had available – at first wood, linen and wool; later, with increasing trade and industrialization, glass, cotton and ceramics.

Sweden's political history has also played its part in the evolution of the country's decorating styles as, over the centuries, periods of economic and political greatness have alternated with far longer periods of national decline.

The evolution of modern Swedish style really begins in the early years of the seventeenth century, when the expansionist king Gustavus Adolphus involved his country in the Thirty Years' War (1618-48). This conflict brought Sweden quite suddenly into contact with the rest of northern European culture. Until that time, Sweden had been regarded as a cultural and political backwater. Now the country became a 'power'.

After the death of Gustavus Adolphus at the Battle of Lützen in 1632, Swedish power and influence continued to grow, as it won tranches of Baltic territories in the peace treaties that were signed at the end of the Thirty Years' War. Increasing wealth attracted painters and architects from Germany, Italy and France to the royal court. Gustavus Adolphus's daughter Christina was only six when her father died, but by the time of her abdication twenty-two years later she headed a court of dazzling Baroque splendour.

In the 1650s, during the reign of Christina's cousin, Carl X Gustav, Nicodemus Tessin (Tessin the Elder) arrived from Germany, the first of three generations of his family to make an indelible impression on Swedish architecture and interior decoration. At this time and for most of the seventeenth century, the Baroque style dominated in Europe and Scandinavia, although Sweden consistently interpreted the style in a lighter, sparer manner and was perhaps less than happy with the heavily ornate manner of her German neighbours. Tessin the Elder's great work is Drottningholm

Palace, built in the 1660s as the royal family's summer palace. Here he successfully and dramatically interwove the European and Scandinavian strands of Baroque style.

This was an age of great castle building, as Swedish nobles sought to underline their new position as a major political force in the Baltic. The austere Skokloster Castle, for instance, was constructed in the 1660s for General Carl Gustav Wrangel on his return home from the wars. Today, the interiors remain more or less intact and are an outstanding example of Swedish Baroque taste. However, Skokloster would have seemed old-fashioned to contemporary French or English eyes. Since there were initially no native architectural styles to follow, its design was based on that of a Polish royal residence built forty years earlier in the 1620s. New styles usually took some time to reach the north at that period.

The late Baroque period and the early Rococo that followed in the first part of the eighteenth century coincided with a reversal in Sweden's fortunes. The wars of the flamboyant warrior king, Carl XII, seriously damaged Sweden's prosperity. The Baltic provinces, so hard-won a century earlier, were lost in the peace treaties signed in 1718. The imperial experiment had failed to give Sweden the security she craved: the loss of territory and the costs of war led to hard economic times and a reaction against autocratic royal rule. Society became polarized, with great riches and power in the hands of a few while the majority lived in conditions of harsh privation.

French-influenced Rococo reigned supreme during the first half of the eighteenth century, at least in the royal residences. A team of French craftsmen under Carl Hårleman (1700-53)

This house, originally used only during summer, has belonged to the same family for many generations. It is now a permanent home, with central heating installed, but still has the feeling of a country summer house. Glazed double doors lead out to a covered porch which provides additional living space in the warmer months. The bare wooden floors, lightly spattered walls and traditional Mora long-case clock are all suggestive of the simple life.

13

ABOVE AND RIGHT *A guest room seen from the hallway of this seventeenth-century hunting lodge north of Stockholm has walls hung with handpainted wallpaper. The detail shows the delicate beauty of the chinoiserie style so popular in the Rococo era in Sweden. This paper, dating from c.1760, was discovered only recently on the backs of the wall panels when they were taken down for restoration. So good was its condition that the panels needed only to be reversed and rehung.*

started work in 1728 on the unfinished interior of the royal palace in Stockholm. But in other circles, for instance among the new-rich merchants and mine-owners, the challenge for Sweden's architects and decorators, both imported and indigenous, was to adapt contemporary taste to the country's straitened circumstances.

Fortunately the newly fashionable Rococo style was lighter and less ornamented than the Baroque, with less gilding, marbling that was more discreet and simpler textiles. These factors made it easier for interior decoration to be pared down: yellow paint could replace gilt on furniture, doors and mirrors; pine floors were satisfactory alternatives to inlay, parquet or marble; furniture was copied from European examples, but designed in such a way that it could be produced by native Swedish furniture-makers. On the walls, even in the wealthiest homes, painted canvas – already popular during the previous century – began to replace rich damask coverings. The increasingly practical, pragmatic Swedish approach to interior design was thoroughly engaged.

But France was not the only influence on interior decoration at the time. The period was one of expanding trade, with imports from Germany, Holland and England also making their mark. Most significantly, though, the Swedish East India Company was set up in 1731 and, like the Dutch and English, Swedish merchants developed a flourishing traffic with the Far East. One of the by-products of this trade was the vogue for chinoiserie that spread throughout Europe. Wallpapers inspired by Chinese wallhangings became fashionable and by 1753, the palace of Drottningholm, in keeping with other palaces and stately homes in Europe, had acquired its own example of Chinese style – a Chinese garden pavilion.

To keep much-needed wealth in the country, the state set up a Manufacturing Office in 1759. Production of Swedish-made articles similar to those being imported was to be encouraged. The Rörstrand faience factory in Stockholm, founded in the 1720s, turned to the making of Chinese-inspired blue and white crockery, sold as an alternative to Far Eastern wares shipped from the Orient. Another of Rörstrand's successes was the manufacture of copies of the then-fashionable German tiled stoves.

Gustavian Style

Named after Gustav III, the Neoclassical manner which developed in the late eighteenth century has become more closely identified with the traditional Swedish look than any other style. Gustav's relatively short reign (1771-92) marked the high point of intellectual and artistic achievement in Sweden. His mother Louisa Ulrika, sister of Frederick the Great of Prussia, had been raised in her brother's highly cultured court and educated the young prince in the spirit of the Age of the Enlightenment. The third Tessin, Carl Gustav, the owner of a magnificent home at Åkerö, which contained one of the very first Neoclassical interiors in Europe, was one of Gustav's tutors and left his mark on the young man's taste.

Gustav developed into a person of immense charm, culture and extravagance. He travelled widely, visiting both France and Italy. In France he was dazzled by the splendour of the court of Louis XV; in Italy he was impressed by the recent archaeological discoveries at Pompeii and Herculaneum. News of these finds spread through Europe, resulting in a taste for the antique which was reflected in austere stonework, classically inspired friezes, medallions, columns and floral swags.

The clean lines of Neoclassicism were much more sympathetic to the indigenous Swedish style than the Baroque or Rococo which, although popular in Sweden, had never really captured the heart of an essentially rural population. The simpler forms of Neoclassicism were altogether more accessible and, what was most important, were relatively inexpensive for provincial painters and craftsmen to imitate.

Gustav III embraced Neoclassicism with enthusiasm. The court he established in Stockholm took the Versailles of Louis XV and Louis XVI as its model, but Swedish Neoclassicism was simpler and more austere, lacking the glitter and gold of its French counterpart. Gustav set himself the task of bringing his palaces and castles up to date, and to assist him he employed two Frenchmen, the architect Louis Jean Desprez and the decorative painter Louis Masreliez. The palace and theatre at Drottningholm were restored and Gustav also planned a massive new palace at Haga, in Pompeiian style. This grand undertaking was never realized, but the Haga pavilion, built to house the king while he supervised the construction work, gives a flavour of what the palace might have looked like.

Designed by Olof Tempelman and decorated by Masreliez, the Haga pavilion was inspired by Le Petit Trianon at Versailles and is a cross between a folly and a palace. The Neoclassical decoration is exquisite, even in the more austere dining room where stonework is suggested by *grisaille* painting of friezes, niches and pediments. At the windows, simple white curtains are hooked delicately back.

Even more representative of the Gustavian style are the courtiers' rooms in the new wing at Gripsholm – until then a gloomy medieval castle. The rooms here, which were restored in the nineteenth century, are decorated with a simple elegance that still looks fresh today. The beds are tented or placed in shallow alcoves, dressed with cotton checks or floral fabrics; the walls are covered in painted canvas. A typical round-backed Gustavian chair stands beside each bed. The whole look is one of economy of style.

Gustav III became increasingly autocratic. Alarmed by the French Revolution, he introduced a state police and tried to undermine the power of his parliament. But his policies failed and he was assassinated by a disaffected aristocrat at the opera in March 1792. His son, Gustav IV Adolf (1792-1809) was deposed in favour of a childless uncle and shortly afterwards, in 1818, Carl XIV Johan, formerly the French marshal Jean-Baptiste Bernadotte, became king of Sweden.

This example of Gustavian style is the result of painstaking restoration. The linen panels were so dirty that the painting on them was barely visible. They were cleaned by the traditional method of rubbing gently with fresh white bread, which absorbs grime without removing the paint. As each room was restored, the owners of the house filled it with period furniture, paintings and decorative objects collected over the years, all of them good examples of their kind and most of them documented. Traditional fabrics were chosen for the furniture; the windows are hung with plain white muslin to let in the light.

Empire to Arts and Crafts

With Bernadotte, a second wave of French influence reached Sweden in the form of the Empire style. This was the style of Napoleon, who dictated how it should be. It was also inspired by antiquity, but prided itself on more authentic detail. The palette of colours was extended to include stronger blues, greens, yellows and reds. Decoration spread to floors: at the Italianate villa of Ekensberg on Lake Mälaren, for example, floorboards were painted to imitate light oak parquet. Walls were more elaborately decorated with painted friezes of Graeco-Roman themes, panels incorporating stylized classical medallions, Roman urns and swords, or elaborate swathes of elegant drapery. Other Empire touches included metal curtain tie-backs in the shape of bunches of grapes or classical masks; Pompeiian-style sofas and chairs; and a greater use of unpainted furniture, rosewood being especially fashionable.

Towards the end of the nineteenth century, the English Arts and Crafts Movement found its way to Sweden, chiefly through the art journal *The Studio*. The main proponents in Sweden, the painter Carl Larsson (1853-1919) and his wife Karin, both read the journal. They made their home at Lilla Hyttnäs, in the province of Dalarna. Larsson's book, *Ett Hem* (A Home), published in 1899, was a charming record of the life of his large family in their red wooden *stuga*, which Karin had inherited. Here, the Larssons grafted the ideals of Gustavian style onto those of the Arts and Crafts Movement. Traditional crafts such as weaving and embroidery and folklore-inspired colours and decoration were all incorporated into a home of Gustavian symmetry and simplicity. The restrictions of historical accuracy which had prevailed earlier in the century were abandoned in favour of an eclectic mixture of styles and periods. The result was an Arts and Crafts style that is singularly Swedish.

Karin's bedroom in the Larssons' home was radically altered to suit the family's requirements. Here Karin's bed can be seen boxed in between the wall and a fitted wardrobe which doubled as a room divider between the mother's sleeping area and her children's cots. The white-washed walls have been simply decorated with painted swags below the green ceiling.

THE ESSENCE OF SWEDISH STYLE

Lessons from the Past

While Carl Larsson's house offers one of the most important sources of inspiration for traditional Swedish style, he was by no means the only person of his time to be concerned with the best of Sweden's past. As early as the 1840s a national handicrafts association had been set up to assemble source materials on which manufacturers could base their designs. The late nineteenth-century king, Carl XV, had his own collection of Renaissance and Baroque furniture and took a keen interest in reviving old arts and crafts. During his reign, work was begun on restoring a number of royal residences, with an eye to recreating their period interiors.

In 1891, Artur Hazelius established the Skansen open-air museum on the island of Djurgården in Stockholm. Though born in the capital, Hazelius had lived for several years in a parsonage in the province of Småland, where he learned much about Sweden's rural past. His extensive journeys through Sweden had also taught him a great deal about the distinctive character of the different regions, and he determined to preserve those local customs and traditions which were being threatened by industrialization and demographic changes. After creating a museum of peasant life in the 1870s, he went on to acquire an extensive site in Stockholm, where he set about rebuilding old farmsteads, erecting them there piece by piece.

Now covering an area of some seventy-five acres (thirty hectares) and containing over 120 buildings, the Skansen Museum remains to this day one of the best places in which to explore traditional Swedish style and to gain an impression of Swedish country crafts in all their variety and vitality. Hazelius was insistent that every building at Skansen should be representative of its period and geographical region. If the logistics of dismantling and re-erecting a specific example he had chosen proved impossible, he preferred to have an accurate copy made rather than nothing at all.

Original exhibits still on show today include the Mora farmstead, acquired in 1885. This is the oldest building at Skansen and is an example of north Swedish rural style. Like so many Swedish farmsteads, it consists of several buildings grouped around a central square yard. Although typical of a seventeenth-century farm, the complex also contains constructions of earlier and later date. The traditional interior features include an open stove with the fire at eye level and beds tucked into curtained alcoves so that the centre of the room is left free for spinning, weaving and a range of other domestic chores.

One of the pearls of the Skansen collection is Skogaholm Manor, an eighteenth-century manor house from Närke. Characteristically, it has a central building limewashed in pale yellow ochre to look like French sandstone. This is flanked by two eighteenth-century wings painted in Falun red (see page 27), which have been refurbished as a kitchen and a suite including library and guest rooms. The interiors of Skogaholm are largely Gustavian, with panelled walls painted in pearl grey or blue, some with *grisaille* decoration. Floorboards are painted grey or to simulate parquet; windows are hung with simple traditional roller blinds; furniture is arranged with customary Gustavian symmetry.

The manor also contains examples of painted faience stoves, stretched canvas painted with Neoclassical detail on the walls, children's beds with simple calico covers and, in the housekeeper's room, crudely stencilled walls typical of such decoration in servants' quarters and rural homes of the time. Guest rooms have distempered walls in yellow. The overall effect is charming.

The Skansen Museum provides a faithful record of rural Swedish life over the past three centuries. Its beautifully preserved interiors are a source of inspiration both to present-day designers and architects and to the many visitors of all nations who admire the intrinsic elegance and inventiveness of traditional Swedish design.

This room in Bollnäs House, a seventeenth-century timber building from the province of Hälsingland, was originally used for entertaining guests. The local painter who decorated the walls in the late eighteenth century based the large trompe-l'oeil *picture above the imitation dado on a biblical theme. The house was among the first buildings to be moved to the Skansen Museum.*

COLOUR AND PAINT

IN A COUNTRY that is dark for half the year, the Swedes have come to appreciate how the clever use of colour can lift the spirits. During the winter, when what little sunshine there is bounces off the snow, subtle Gustavian whites and greys help to maximize that light. Rustic styles and colours of painting on walls and furniture add warmth and humour to the home, and the clear yellows, blues and greens of painted walls are reminders of summer.

Paint is used everywhere in the Swedish home – inside and out, on walls, ceilings, window frames and doors, wooden panelling, furniture, fireplaces and accessories. The versatility of paint – the fact that it can be used on so many different types of surface to create an instant impact – has always suited Swedish decorating needs perfectly. And the traditional media, in which the craftsmen of past centuries worked, have an attractive subtlety of colour and texture which no modern paint can emulate.

The distemper commonly used for painting interior walls and ceilings, whether plastered or wooden, was made from powdered chalk or whiting, water, glue (often animal or bone glue, called

In a country house, the exposed timber walls of the guest room have been painted a similar greyish blue to the rest of the woodwork and some of the furniture. The restful tone is repeated in the furnishing fabrics and the rag rug, as well as some of the accessories. A brighter blue on the bench to the left, a colour found on many pieces of old Swedish furniture, has been weathered by age to a soft finish in keeping with the room's overall atmosphere.

size) and powdered pigments. For plain painting it was brushed on thickly with a large brush, but it could also be employed for many of the more elaborate paint techniques that were used so extensively in the late eighteenth and early nineteenth centuries in Sweden.

Distemper gives a somewhat fragile finish that rubs off comparatively easily, so it is surprising that so many old examples of distempered finishes remain in Sweden today. For a more durable but far more costly finish, for instance on furniture or on their painted canvas wallhangings, the Swedes favoured egg tempera. This very old type of paint is made from water, linseed oil and pigment combined with egg yolk. The paint takes a long time to dry, but the surface it forms is tough and long-lasting. Though expensive, egg tempera is still in demand today for delicate decorative work.

Oil-based paint also found favour in Sweden as it did throughout the rest of Europe, and was certainly in use by the seventeenth century. Since flax was a staple product of the country, the linseed oil needed to make it was widely available. Although regarded as expensive, it was still cheaper than egg tempera and dried faster, but was equally durable and had an attractive sheen. Oil paint was commonly used for furniture in the eighteenth century, though the specific pearl-grey finish associated with Gustavian furniture is now thought to be something of a myth. Restorers have stripped layers of oil paint off this furniture until they reached a grey paint presumed to be the original finished surface, but which in fact is the original lead white undercoat. This white undercoat might

have had some black pigment added to compensate for the yellowing that occurs with lead white, and it would also have discoloured as succeeding layers of oil paint were added. The resulting grey may not have been the original surface, but it has now become common to regard it as such. And why not? It may not be historically authentic, but it is certainly most attractive and without doubt suits the lines of Gustavian furniture.

Today distemper is regaining its previous popularity in Sweden. This is partly because, as a water-based paint without potentially harmful solvents among its ingredients, it is considered ecologically sound; but partly also because it offers an attractive alternative to the flat hard finish of emulsion [latex] paint. The slightly weathered, aged look that can be achieved with this traditional paint makes it a good choice for anyone wishing to restore an old house without the overall effect appearing too crisp and modern.

There are now specialist stockists of both distempers and oil-based paints in suitable historically accurate colours. Distempers can be supplied in ready-made form or in a powder to be made up as required. It is not too difficult to colour your own, adding powder pigments or stainers of your choice; but remember that the dry finish will be much paler than the wet paint.

As well as creating a soft plain surface, distemper is also suited to a number of decorative paint techniques, including spattering, marbling and stencilling, which are characteristic of Scandinavian interiors. Much used in past centuries, these techniques will help to give your home the traditional Swedish look.

COLOUR AND PAINT

The Exterior

In Sweden one of the most important readily available building materials has always been timber, used for all but the grandest residences. However, in a climate of long, freezing winters and short, warm summers, wooden houses require protection from the elements. Paint provides that protection admirably.

LEFT *The soft green windows and shutters of this seventeenth-century house offer an intriguing contrast to the deep yellow walls.*

BELOW *On timber houses the rich tones of Falun red provide a warm background that goes equally well with front doors painted in a fresh blue or a strong ochre.*

For exteriors the Swedes have long used a traditional limewash. This was mixed with a range of pigments, often the earth shades, to give a bright, translucent colour that is particularly enhanced by the Swedish light. Made of slaked lime and water and painted directly onto a dry plastered wall, limewash in effect coats the surface with a thin, hard layer of lime. It also acts as a disinfectant so was used annually in many stables and outhouses. For older houses, limewash offers better exterior protection than modern paints since it allows the walls to breathe, rather than sealing in the damp. As there are certain health hazards associated with using limewash it is important to obtain specialist advice before trying it.

Nowadays timber farmsteads painted Falun red are a distinguishing feature of much of Sweden's countryside. Originally produced from the waste of the copper mines at Falun in the province of Dalarna, this pigment was once also used by the upper classes for the exteriors of their homes. The red walls of wooden *stugor* and farmhouses make a dramatic contrast with the crisp white of their doors and shutters and with bright winter snow.

Manor houses may be painted in a subtle shade of buttermilk yellow to make believe they are made of yellow sandstone. Rich tawny pink and muted orange limewashes add an almost Mediterranean warmth and vibrancy to many Swedish townscapes.

A Changing Palette

Historically, the range of colours used by traditional painters and decorators in Sweden was determined to some extent by the types of paint available. Certain pigments, for example, are not compatible with the limewash used for exterior walls, and this limited the range of colours seen on the outsides of stone and timber buildings. Neither were all pigments equally easy to obtain. While some occurred naturally in local minerals or could be derived from native plants, others had to be imported and in times of economic decline or war their supply became erratic. Although a number of pigments, such as white lead, had been manufactured for several centuries, the advent of the industrial revolution and the development of more sophisticated technology increased the range of colours being made.

In the seventeenth century, when Baroque fashions prevailed, the dominant colours of the Swedish palette were deep greens and blues, some red, and a lot of gold. These rich colours were the perfect foil to the heavy textiles and embossed and gilded wallcoverings that were popular then, and to the *grisaille* painting and marbling (see pages 34, 51-3) that often accompanied them. The overall effect was one of heavy, almost oppressive opulence.

The early eighteenth century brought with it from France the influence of the Rococo style. Now the palette became much lighter and more feminine, with colours such as grey, mid-blue, pale clear green, straw yellow and pink prevailing. Gilding became less important. The arrival of Rococo style coincided with a decline in Sweden's fortunes, so it was fortunate for the Swedes that the extravagances of the Baroque period had passed. The new colours could be mixed with less concentrated pigment and so were less expensive to produce. Where a gilded effect was desired, yellow paint was used instead of gold leaf.

The Gustavian palette did not differ much from the Rococo palette, but there was a change in the style of painting. Decoration became much more pared-down and spare, often inspired by Classical detailing. The look was one of restrained elegance and symmetry. Towards the end of the century some stronger colours returned to favour, but now they were used as occasional touches against predominantly pale shades, rather than as the dominant colours in a decorating scheme.

This was also a time when painted furniture became very popular, in colours such as clear grey, deep sky blue and corn yellow. The preferred medium for furniture was oil-based paint, which gave a paler, subtler colour than the gesso layers that had been popular with the Rococo style.

The Empire period at the beginning of the nineteenth century brought with it a range of much stronger colours, often used in unusual contrasting combinations. Maroon was combined with grey-green, yellow ochre with dark blue, grey with bright green, green with gold. Once again, the effect was rich and sumptuous, giving the sense of an empire basking in its wealth and glory.

In the later nineteenth century many homes in Sweden as well as elsewhere in Europe adopted dark, sombre colour schemes sometimes combined with an excess of heavy furniture. Browns, maroons and dark greens were fashionable then, the result of the newly discovered aniline dyes.

The effect of the Arts and Crafts movement at the turn of the century was to help shake off this gloom. In Sweden, under the influence of Carl Larsson, a peculiarly Swedish form of Arts and Crafts style emerged. This combined the simplicity and symmetry of Gustavian style with the colours and decorating traditions previously found in rural cottages and farms.

The pale colours associated with Swedish decorating style were usually complemented by pale flooring. Floorboards were traditionally left bare rather than painted. Deal boards scoured with diluted caustic soda, lightly sanded and finished with a protective layer of soft soap, provided a bleached lightness just as attractive as floors painted in pastel shades, but a great deal easier to maintain.

RIGHT *In the parlour of the Ekshärad house at Skansen, the walls are painted in yellow distemper above the dado, and in grey below it.*

OVERLEAF *The strong colours which were popularized by the Arts and Crafts movement work well both in the orthodox treatment of woodwork in a farmhouse kitchen, and in the less conventional combination of bright green ceiling and electric blue banisters with white walls and door used for a small entrance hall.*

CHOOSING PALETTES

One of the most obvious characteristics of the Swedish look is the colour palette, particularly the range used for paint. Although there are no hard and fast rules, the two types of palette shown here, the rural and the Gustavian, are definitely the most popular. Both are based on colours that are clear and never muddy, but the reds, greens and yellows derived from traditional country cottage exteriors are more brilliant and saturated. Gustavian colours, by comparison, are more muted and chalky, with soft pastels and greyish whites predominating.

However, you do not have to stick too narrowly to one type or the other. Gentle hues mix well with bolder ones. A pale grey or lavender wall, for example, can be an excellent foil for a pair of chairs painted in the more assertive blue commonly seen on eighteenth-century furniture. Remember, too, that in Swedish interiors the texture of the painted finish is rarely flat and uniform as it is in many modern homes in other parts of the world. Whichever palette has been chosen, the effects of wear and tear, of sunlight and of different paint media all add a further dimension to the basic colour.

Decorative Techniques

At the Swedish court and among wealthy families, foreign or foreign-educated architects, designers and painters were often employed and they imported the latest decorating styles, chiefly from France and Italy. For grander projects they might even bring with them foreign carpenters, decorators and carvers trained in particular styles. These craftsmen then took their ideas beyond the capital, working for wealthy families and teaching their skills to Swedes.

Inventive decorative techniques have always been a feature in Swedish homes, where the *faux* finish has long been used to great effect. When only the richest could afford to use the very limited supplies of indigenous stone, or to buy costly Italian marble, and when rich textiles and furniture were the preserve of the few, the resourceful Swedes turned naturally to paint to create the illusion of wealth. As the opulent Baroque style spread through Europe in the seventeenth century, Swedish painter/decorators began to excel at various forms of *trompe l'oeil*. They painted stretched linen wall panels to look like rich Gobelins tapestry; they used various paint techniques to imitate the marble and stone they could not afford to import and the plasterwork that was too expensive to execute.

During the eighteenth century much use was made of *grisaille*, a type of monochrome *trompe l'oeil* effect. Applied to ceilings, wall and door panels, covings and cornices it gave the appearance of carved wood or plasterwork. It could also imitate Neoclassical cast decoration, stonework, friezes, roundels, insets and even triumphal swags. Often, even fireplaces and chimney pieces were painted to resemble stone, then decorated with classically inspired motifs. *Grisaille* takes its name from the French *gris* meaning grey, because it is most often worked in grey paint with white highlights, although sometimes green or brown were also used.

LEFT *Fake architectural features were not confined to the palace and manor house. Here a dado has been painted straight onto the wooden walls of a modest hallway.*

RIGHT *The walls of the parlour in this manor house have been painted a soothing blue-green and decorated with simple rectangles of faux moulding above a simulated dado in order to create a formal note.*

BORDERS AND PANELLING

Painted borders and panels offer a precise way of dividing up walls that appeals to the Swedish love of symmetry and order. Divisions could be made either horizontally, in the form of dado, filling and frieze, or vertically, by the use of panels framing a doorway, window or tiled stove. Rather than adding carved wooden moulding or ornamental plasterwork, the effect could be achieved more easily and at far less expense with paint.

The simplest type of division consisted of straight lines, painted singly or in pairs. The area between the lines might be filled in with a toning colour or with a Greek key design, or the lines themselves might be embellished with floral swags. *Trompe l'oeil* laurel leaf borders were another popular choice. The motifs used varied from detailed and accurate copies of classical motifs or botanically correct French-influenced flower designs in the homes of the nobles, to simpler, charming, if cruder, floral garlands on the walls of the less well-off. Sometimes the designs were applied directly to the wood panelling of the walls, but they were often painted onto linen or canvas panels that could be changed to suit the latest fashion.

LEFT *A border of leaves trails across the top of boarded doors fitted with an exaggeratedly low dado.*

RIGHT *In the newly decorated bedroom of an old manor house, the borders of the main panels are painted in a bright blue glaze.*

OVERLEAF *A medley of borders, garlands and panels from which to draw inspiration.*

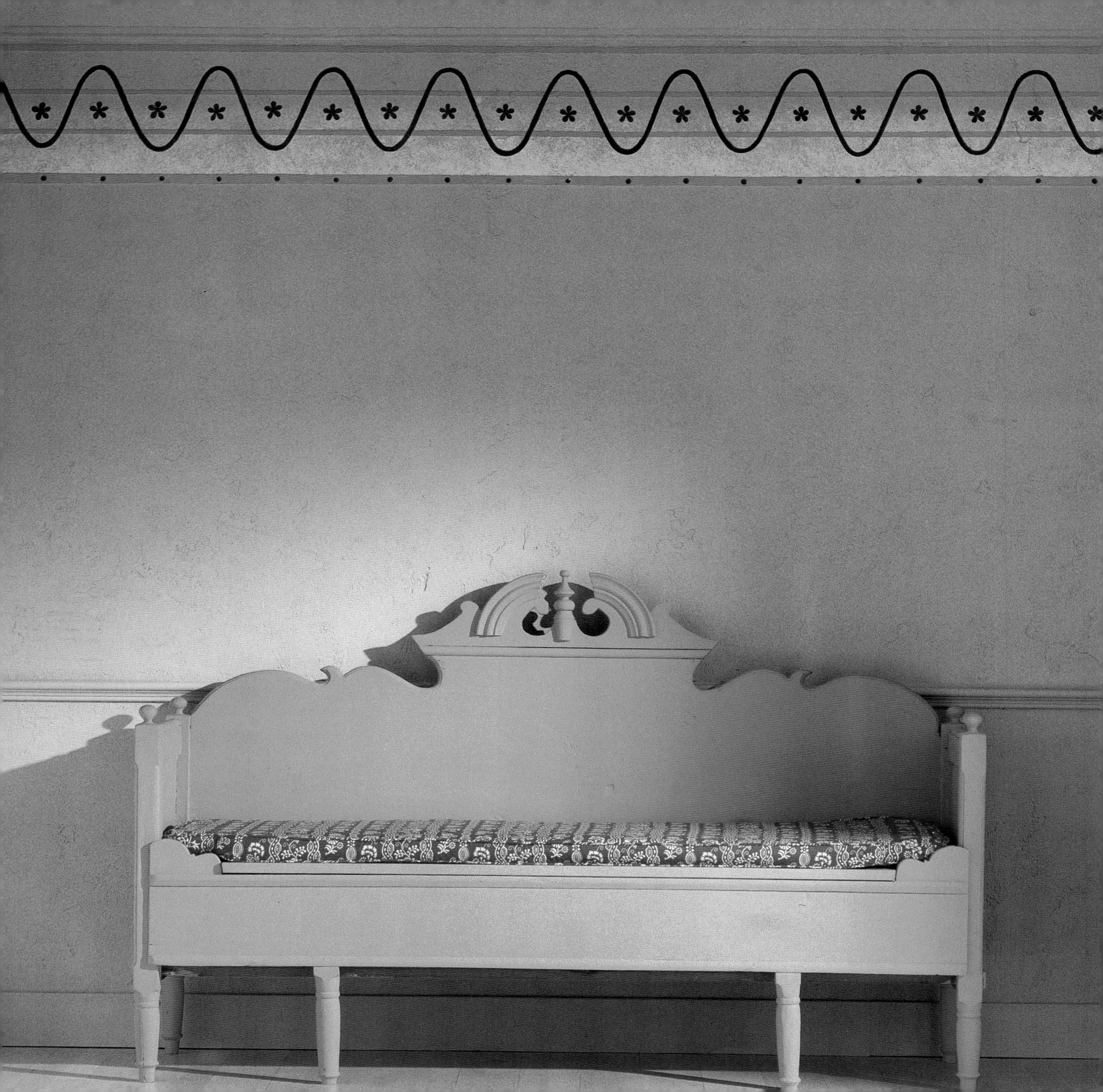

A RUSTIC BORDER

A room painted with this border would need very little other decoration.
Capturing the whimsy and humour of Swedish paint effects, the border looks complicated
but is actually quite simple to achieve.

PLANNING THE LAYOUT

1 Painting this border requires careful advance planning. Measure the height of your room: the design shown here is 52cm/20in deep on a 2.4m/8ft ceiling, but you may have to adjust it while retaining the relative proportions to suit the dimensions of your room. Experiment by marking the lower edge of the border in pencil to see if the proportions look right before you go ahead. Measure the width of the walls. You need to ensure that each curved line reaches a corner at either the highest or lowest part of its curve, and that the curved line on the next wall starts at the corresponding point. This may mean adjusting the vertical spacing of the whole design.

MARKING OUT THE DESIGN

2 Using a large decorator's brush, apply two thin coats of pale grey paint to the walls and allow to dry.

3 Measure 52cm/20in from the ceiling or cornice and, using a tape measure and straightedge, draw a horizontal pencil line parallel with the ceiling. Draw a second line 18cm/7in above that, another 14cm/5½in above that and another 17cm/6½in above that. These mark the base lines of the bands of colour (a).

4 Measure and mark the thickness of the lines. The lowest and highest bands of colour should be 25mm/1in wide and those in the middle 12mm/½in wide.

5 Mask off the grey-painted area below the lowest line and water down some white paint using one part water to three parts paint. Working from the masking tape upwards, gently and evenly sponge the wall, graduating the sponging away to nothing just above the second line (b). Remove the masking tape while the paint is still wet and allow to dry.

a

b

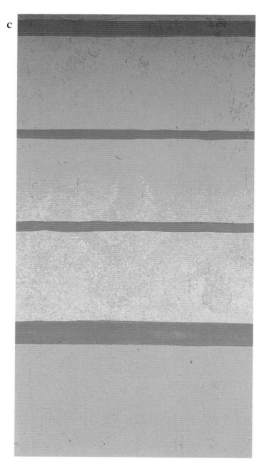

PAINTING THE YELLOW LINES

6 When the sponged coat is dry, start with the space adjoining the ceiling and work downwards, painting in the yellow lines with a 12mm/½in brush (c). This can be done by masking off above and below the areas to be painted, but painting them freehand gives a more rustic feel. Freehand painting requires a steady hand, so it is a good idea to practise first on a piece of board before tackling the wall. Leave to dry completely.

PAINTING THE SECOND COLOUR

7 Make a pencil mark dot every 15cm/ 6in along the bottom yellow line. Using a straightedge and spirit level measure vertically upwards from these points to mark a second row of dots in the middle of the centre broad band. This second row of dots gives the positions for the centre of the small petalled flowers.

8 Using an artist's brush, paint the dots in rust brown paint on the bottom yellow line to form rough circles of about 12mm/ ½in diameter. Using the same brush and colour, paint the petalled flowers freehand (d). Leave to dry completely.

9 Using a pencil, mark a dot alternately directly above and below each flower (e). You should end up with a row of dots in the centre of the white sponged band and another row in the first broad band beneath ceiling level. Using a pencil, join these marks in a curved zig-zag to give one edge of the rust brown line. For the second, outside edge, mark then join another set of dots 12mm/½in from the first line.

10 To complete the design, paint between the two pencilled curves using the rust brown paint and an artist's brush (right).

PANELLING WITH GARLANDS

*This pretty design takes its inspiration from the decorative panels
found at Gripsholm. The simple framework of painted panels above a dado
is embellished with twining leaves, scattered with bell flowers.*

MATERIALS AND EQUIPMENT

Matt water-based paints:
Pale blue
Medium blue
Dark blue
Dark grey-blue
Dark oxblood red
Light pink
Medium pink
White

Decorator's brushes
Artist's brushes
Tape measure or ruler
Straightedge
Pencil
Natural sponge

a

b

PREPARATION
1 Make sure that the wall surface is clean and dust free. Paint the whole wall pale blue, applying two thin coats.

PLANNING THE LAYOUT
2 When the base coat is dry, lightly pencil in the outlines of the panels. Divide each wall into single or triple panels above a painted dado, according to the shape of the room. There are no hard and fast rules about proportion, and it is usually a case of using your eye to determine the most pleasing design.

PAINTING THE DESIGN
3 Paint the panel surround (the stiles and rails) medium blue. When this has dried, paint the panel outlines and dado line dark blue, preferably freehand to give a slightly rustic look **(a)**.

4 Pencil in a line approximately 15cm/6in inside the inner panel, and paint it oxblood red **(b)**.

c

d

THE GARLAND

5 Lightly draw the garland in pencil, starting with the laurel wreath in the centre of the bottom line. Making sure the corners match, twine the garland symmetrically around the red line. Draw in the leaves, starting from the bottom centre and working towards each corner of the panel and up to and across the top. Vary the shapes and sizes of the leaves, adding short vine tendrils and curled up leaves at random. This design combines elements from different plants. Aim for a result that is visually and artistically pleasing, rather than botanically accurate.

6 Using medium blue and a thin soft artist's brush, paint in the stems, leaves and tendrils **(c)**.

7 Using the dark grey-blue, add a few veins to the leaves and some random drop shadows. Paint the little bell flowers in light pink, arranging them in clusters at irregular intervals. Add some shadows and details in medium pink **(d)**.

8 Mix a little white paint with water and dip the natural sponge into it, wringing it out thoroughly. Very lightly sponge over the whole area, including the middle of the panel, to create a chalky and uneven antique finish.

Rustic Decoration

ABOVE *Two rooms painted by Jonas Hertman in the late eighteenth century. The zig-zag pattern imitates Hungarian needlepoint hangings while the fish-scale pattern is derived from seventeenth-century woollen textiles.*

RIGHT *The floral decoration on this dresser dates from the 1820s. The Tree of Life visible in the far room was a popular* kurbits *motif.*

While decorating styles came and went among court circles and the upper middle classes, rural styles of decorating and the palette of colours used in peasant homes remained more or less the same. Until the early nineteenth century most members of the peasant class could not afford anything other than the most basic sort of home, and here decoration would have been limited to what could be achieved cheaply and easily. But by the middle of the century, the peasants in those parts of Sweden – Dalarna, Hälsingland and Gästrikland – that had become wealthy through the sale of copper, iron, flax and timber, were able to afford well-built, sturdy timber homes and had the means to decorate them well.

The nineteenth century also saw a shift in taste. Paint techniques became more individual and idiosyncratic: sponging, spattering and marbling remained popular but were used less and less to look like natural materials, and more for the entertainment value they gave. To a certain extent these paint effects were a means of showing off – proving to your neighbours that you could afford to employ a painter. A number of the more rough and ready examples, however, suggest that some homemakers tried their hand at painting themselves.

Many professional painters were itinerant workers, who introduced more fanciful forms of decoration to different parts of the country as they travelled. Unlike the artists working for wealthy clients, very few of them are known by name, but they were responsible for the diffusion of a strong, vivacious rural style known as *kurbits* painting. The word *kurbits* means gourd or pumpkin, and the motif was often included in depictions of festoons of fruit and flowers. During the summer the painters would wander the country looking for work for the coming winter, carrying with them samples of what they could do. They used whatever materials were available locally: coal, clay, soot and the juices of berries as colouring agents; skimmed or sour milk, beer or vinegar as a binder; water, soft soap, *snaps* and even urine as the medium. Their commissions came from both the Church and secular employers, and they often took religious motifs into private homes or court motifs into outlying areas.

The *kurbits* painters could turn their hand to anything – biblical themes, imitation wallhangings painted on coarse linen in the style of the court painters, townscape motifs inspired by the French pictorial wallpapers that were fashionable among the richer classes. Sometimes their work included allusions to jokes or to family events, and characters would be depicted with 'speech bubbles' coming from their mouths. Nor was the *kurbits* style confined to the walls. It was also used to great effect on furniture.

Farmhouse interiors were less subdued than courtly homes. While elaborate painting tended to be reserved for living rooms, the travelling painters decorated hallways and kitchens with marbling, stencilling or spatter painting, all useful techniques to cover the walls of timber buildings whose cracks could not readily be concealed with expensive wallpapers.

These spatter painted wooden walls date from the late nineteenth century and can be seen in the Ekshärad house at the Skansen Museum. The two additional colours have been applied very sparingly so that they add little more than a subtle contrast to the solid base paint. Spattering the paint from birch twigs creates larger, more random flecks of colour than using a brush. The traditional technique used a different bunch of twigs for each colour.

SPATTERING

Typically Swedish, spatter painting was popular at every level of society. In the homes of nobles, it might well be used to reproduce the effect of porphyry on the base of a column or on a plinth or bench top. Porphyry is a heavy, sombre stone that comes in nearly 300 different colorations. Sweden was the only country in Europe where deposits had been found. Difficult to quarry and shape and therefore expensive, it is not surprising that artists sought ways to imitate it.

In less affluent homes, spattering was used with more light-hearted freedom on both walls and furniture. On walls it could often be seen on a dado, with stencilled designs above, or in combination with marbling. On furniture it was sometimes used to add an element of surprise, for example inside a cupboard door.

Spattering has always been very simple and cheap to do. The traditional method is to flick two or three distemper tints onto a distemper base with birch twigs. The look produced could range from bold rustic simplicity to a much more subtle finish. Colours could be quiet – black, greys and whites – or quite dramatic, for example spatters of white and black over a maroon-red base. The effect of spattering changes according to the density of the spots of paint: when the spatters are applied sparingly and irregularly so that a lot of the base colour shows through, the spattering simply softens the appearance of the solid coat of distemper beneath. But to achieve an effect that more closely resembles a stone such as porphyry, the spatters must be applied more densely and evenly, and appropriate colours must be used.

MARBLING

Marbling has been popular in Europe since the time of the Romans. It was certainly one of the most popular paint effects in Sweden from the seventeenth century onwards. Examples are evident everywhere: in houses large and small, on fireplaces and doors, on chairs and on table and chest tops. They vary in sophistication, although, on the whole, Swedish marbling tends to be less naturalistic than that carried out in Italy, for the very good reason that there are few local examples to copy.

Marbling, whether you are aiming at a naturalistic or a fantasy effect, is quick to do once you have the knack. The result often gives a warmer, more comfortable look than the real thing. Before beginning work, study several kinds of marble to familiarize yourself with the way the veins run and criss-cross, and with the combination of thinner bands of veining with finer, secondary veins. The range of different types of marble is huge: black marble with gold veining; rose marble with pink and brown; white carrara marble with its distinctive rippling veins.

Start by applying a base coat, then a glaze coat onto which you paint different colours mixed with glaze to simulate the veins in the marble. According to the type of marble you wish to copy, the veins may be added with a fine artist's brush, a medium-sized decorator's brush or even feathers, pieces of cut sponge, or crumpled paper or rag. Once the veins have been painted, their edges are immediately softened with a dusting brush or lint-free cloth. The finished surface should then be allowed to dry thoroughly, before being given two or three coats of varnish.

ABOVE *In the entrance hall to the Ekshärad house, the pattern has been continued across the wooden wall and the door. This bold interpretation of a marble surface looks more like a random abstract pattern than stone. The painters had often rarely seen examples of real marble, and they allowed their imaginations to run wild.*

OVERLEAF *Two further examples of marbling from the same house have been painted directly onto the wooden walls, probably using distemper. The strong colours and large scale of the veining are wonderfully adventurous and free. In the picture on the left, circular rings of rye bread have been threaded through wooden poles to dry.*

STENCILLING

Stencilling is one of the easiest ways of adding repeat decoration to a surface, requiring no greater skill than a steady hand and a thick, quick-drying paint. It was a decorative technique that was popular in Sweden, both in farmhouses and cottages, and in the grander manor houses. Stencilling was first used by the Swedes to decorate churches in the Middle Ages, before being employed in the house. It declined in popularity in the 1700s when a freer, softer style of painting was preferred, but came back into fashion in the nineteenth century. Stencilled patterns in distemper, tempera and oil paints could be found on almost every surface, from walls, floors and ceilings to

BELOW *This colourful stencilled wall is in the entrance hall of an old farmstead, now one of the exhibits in the Skansen Museum. It was painted straight onto the wood around 1837 by two men from Dalarna, a province renowned throughout Sweden for the skill of its itinerant decorative painters.*

furniture. Even when wallpaper became popular and furniture was being grained, the Swedes could not do without their stencils and started to use them on top of the graining and on roller blinds and doors. The designs included garlands of flowers, urns, geometric figures, trees and imitations of expensive wallpapers or brocade wallhangings. On the floors of grander homes, stencilling was sometimes used to create the impression of the all-over pattern of a carpet.

The whole range of typical Swedish colours was employed, often deriving their impact from the strong contrast between, say, maroon stencilled on pearl grey, rusty red on yellow ochre, or blue on off-white or soft pink.

BELOW *When redecorating this guest room in a house outside Stockholm, the owners found traces of an earlier stencil pattern. They cut new stencils and restored the room to its former appearance, using the same muted tones to create an overall effect that mimics patterned wallpaper.*

A FARMHOUSE STENCIL

This simple two-colour stencil – an adaptation of a mid nineteenth-century pattern from a farmhouse in Hälsingland – cleverly conveys the impression of an elaborate pattern.

MATERIALS AND EQUIPMENT

Matt water-based paints:
Pale grey-blue
Dark grey-blue
Red

Decorator's, artist's and
stencil brushes
Tape measure or ruler
Masking tape
Straightedge
Spirit level
Pencil and chalk
Tracing and carbon paper
Stencil card
Scalpel or craft knife

PLANNING THE LAYOUT

1 When stencilling a whole room, first decide which is the dominant, or most visible wall. This may be the wall facing the door, or the one containing the chimney breast. Aim to make your stencil design an exact horizontal fit along this and the facing wall. Unless your room is square, the stencil design may not fit the other two walls exactly. You may be left with an incomplete pattern in the corners unless you make minor adjustments to the grid by widening it at regular intervals to ensure a precise fit. To find the width that your stencil needs to be, divide the width of the wall by the number of times you wish the design to repeat. If the stencil does not exactly fit the height of the wall, it is usually best to have a complete stencil at the top and incomplete patterns at dado or floor level.

PREPARATION

2 Using a large decorator's brush apply two thin coats of pale grey-blue paint.

MARKING OUT A GRID

3 Create a grid consisting of a series of boxes the exact size of the inner rectangle of stencil A (overleaf). Measure horizontally along the top of the wall to find the centre. Using a spirit level and straightedge, chalk a vertical line from top to bottom. Work outwards from here marking all the vertical lines in chalk. Then mark in all the horizontal lines, working from top to bottom (a, overleaf).

Stencil A

STENCILLING

5 If you are right-handed, start in the top right-hand corner of the principal wall. Start in the top left-hand corner if you are left-handed. Align the triangles of **Stencil A** with the corners of the first rectangle and secure with masking tape. Dip the stencil brush lightly into the dark grey-blue paint, brushing off the excess with a rag. Gently tap the brush over the stencil. To minimize the chance of smearing the paint, stencil alternate rectangles along the top row, then miss the second row and continue stencilling alternate boxes along the next row down. Continue to the lowest row, and when the paint has dried fill in the gaps until you have completed the first stencil (**b**).

a

CUTTING THE STENCILS

4 Using tracing paper, trace off the two designs **A** and **B**. Scale them up on a photocopier to your chosen size. Using carbon paper transfer each stencil onto a piece of stencil paper slightly larger than the design, making sure there is an even border on all four sides. The dimensions of the example shown here are 24 x 19cm/9½ x 7½in, but you should adjust the size to suit the dimensions of your room. Using a scalpel or craft knife, carefully cut the pattern for each stencil. You will need a few copies of each stencil, as they become saturated with paint and require time to dry. Cut a small triangle into each corner of **Stencil A** and notches into the edges of **Stencil B** as shown. These are to help with alignment on the wall, and do not form part of the design.

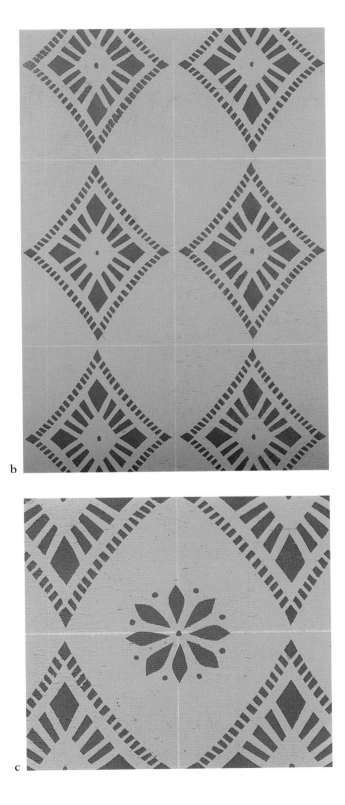

b

c

6 Starting again in the top-right corner of the principal wall, centre **Stencil B** over the point where the vertical and horizontal lines cross, aligning the notches in the stencil with the chalk lines, and secure with masking tape. Dip the cleaned stencil brush into the red paint, and stencil along the wall using the same method as the first stencil, once again working alternately so as not to smudge the paint (**c**).

7 When the whole design has been filled in and the paint has dried, use a damp cloth to wipe away the chalk lines. Fill in any missed parts of the pattern with a small brush. Continue the process for the other walls in the room.

FLÖTJAN

NÄSKUBBEN

HUVUDSKÄR

Sv. HÖGARNA

FURNITURE

A SWEDISH ROOM is never static: furniture is designed to be moved around as required. The look is one of calm spaciousness and pleasing proportions. An empty space is left alone if it does not need filling. Furniture is used sparsely, even in the wealthiest of homes, and depends for its effect on placement. Just as the eye is carried from room to room, so in each room it will come to rest on a few well-chosen and carefully arranged pieces. The fashion for placing furniture against the walls, to leave the centre of the room free, adds to the sense of space and is easy to copy.

Much Swedish furniture shows an in-escapable sense of playfulness. Sideboards with doors beneath a glass-fronted cabinet might have a further series of small drawers hidden away inside. Legends, family names and initials are inscribed on cupboards, drawers and doors, personalizing furniture that was specially made and painted for the household. Even on an austere Gustavian piece there might be a small area of light-hearted carving.

Over the centuries, Swedish furniture has been subject to many influences. Of these, one of the earliest stems from the indigenous rural tradition – heavy-duty, simple wooden furniture made by local craftsmen that was often embellished with

In the large formal dining room of a period country hunting lodge, this wooden sideboard holds the table linen and silver. Its straight, almost severe lines are relieved by the graceful curves and scrolls of the carved lyre motif on the doors, which are echoed in the decorative back. The piece is painted in a typically Gustavian pastel shade.

carving and painted decoration according to the means of the owner. The colours used were largely strong, dark shades – reds derived from inexpensive iron oxides, greens and deep blues.

Other influences came from abroad. In the seventeenth century, the west coast around Göteborg, being closest to England and Holland, was particularly susceptible to English and Dutch styles. Hardwoods such as rosewood and mahogany were much in evidence. In the 1680s, straight, high-backed chairs of turned and carved wood, sometimes with caned seats and backs clearly derived from Dutch or English design, were produced and many such chairs were imported. Cabinets were frequently copied from German or Dutch designs or, again, were imported. The early eighteenth century brought the softer, more rounded lines of the Rococo – simple cabriole legs, sinuous armrests and curved backrests as well as chests with comfortable, rounded bellies.

The grandeur of the French courts of Louis XV and Louis XVI that Desprez introduced to the royal court at Stockholm was quickly adapted by indigenous Swedish craftsmen for use in the homes of those outside the royal circle. The more homely approach of Swedish craftsmen knocked the *hauteur* from French style. The result was a very recognizably Swedish type of furniture. The elaborate curves and flourishes of gessoed Rococo chairs and tables were toned down and simplified, and gilding was kept to a minimum. Even the leaner Neoclassical style of the late eighteenth century was pared down still further, leaving furniture with a purer, straighter line enhanced by simple paintwork in pale colours – white,

pale blue, soft greens and creamy yellows, and the ubiquitous pearl grey. This elegant fusion of Swedish taste with imported ideas resulted in the Gustavian style, which continues to exert a major influence on present-day design.

Beyond the circle of the court, necessity was very much the mother of invention. In the king's palaces, sofas and chairs would have been upholstered in silk brocades and damasks, just as at any other European royal residence. To protect such costly textiles, the furniture was given loose covers made from linen and calico. The simple printed or woven checked or striped fabric then gradually crept into general use as the everyday upholstery of those lower down the social scale, in parsonages and manor houses.

The simpler lines of Gustavian furniture not only suited the more modest Swedish taste but were also easier to produce from softwood. Because pine was virtually the only wood available, Swedish craftsmen would often paint it, both to conceal its humble origins and to add variety to its appearance. For this reason painted furniture has always been important in Sweden but it really came into its own in the late eighteenth century. Some of the simply painted Gustavian furniture is sublime and has stood the test of time very well, looking good to a modern eye attuned to minimal decoration. Craftsmen traditionally ground the pigments by hand, producing a powder with grains that were larger and more light reflective than mechanically emulsified pigment, and the finished effect is one of subtle beauty.

The simple lines of Gustavian furniture make it suitable for use in every room. A pair of dining chairs look just as good flanking a chest of drawers beneath a living-room window as they do round the dining table. A small table with a marbled top can equally well be used as an elegant writing table or as a bedside table. Many pieces fulfil one or more functions. Tables double as sideboards, benches as beds. To maximize the space, beds are often made to extend lengthways or sideways, and dining tables can fold away to stand unobtrusively against the wall.

The Gustavian style also emphasized the use of symmetry in the arrangement of furniture. A stove in one corner of a room would be mirrored by a cupboard in the opposite corner painted to look like a matching stove. This feeling for symmetry can easily be copied by modern decorators seeking to achieve the classic Swedish look.

With the early nineteenth century came the Biedermeier and Empire styles, from Germany and France respectively. Both of these were also adapted to suit Swedish taste. Native woods such as birch and beech proved an attractive, light-coloured substitute for the rosewood and maple that predominated in Germany and France, while the sometimes grand proportions of Biedermeier furniture were scaled down to suit the smaller rooms in Swedish homes.

In the late nineteenth and early twentieth centuries, the Arts and Crafts movement, whose best-known Swedish exponent was Carl Larsson, brought a revolt against the cluttered look of the mid-century. There was a renewed insistence on simplicity. Rustic crafts were also revived, and utilitarian furniture painted in the traditional reds, greens and blues found favour again.

ABOVE *This carved antique sideboard, with a pale distressed paint finish, is flanked by two symmetrically arranged painted chairs.*

LEFT *The top of this small octagonal pedestal side table has been painted with a marbled finish to add a naive charm to an otherwise slightly sombre piece of furniture.*

RIGHT *A pair of comfortable Gripsholm chairs in unpainted wood have been upholstered in the yellow checked linen typical of Swedish traditional style.*

Benches and Sofas

LEFT *This comfortable corner bench makes good use of space in a square room without sacrificing beauty. The Swedish-made tea table based on an English style seems much more sensible than a low coffee table.*

BELOW *Practicality is often the key to Swedish design. This quaint little bench, for example, is an ideal place to sit while putting on shoes. When it is no longer needed, it folds up inconspicuously against the wall.*

Traditional carved and painted wooden benches can still be found throughout Sweden in all types of home. In a rustic setting they can be used for seating in conjunction with dining tables. With cushions and loose upholstery they become bench sofas – a feature of most kitchens in Sweden – somewhere comfortable where people can relax, making the kitchen cosy and intimate.

The corner sofa is really an extension of the bench sofa. It is an extremely popular item in Swedish homes, and provides a good example of the adaptability of their furniture: it looks equally appropriate in the kitchen, dining room or sitting room and is practical where space is limited.

Fat, squashy sofas have always been uncongenial to Swedish taste; the typical Swedish-style sofa evolved from the country bench during the reign of Gustav III. The result is a low, elegant, understated piece of furniture, with a straight, often balustraded back. Three or four pairs of legs support the seat. These legs might be classically square and reeded, or decorated with small carved medallions; they might be the sabre legs of the early nineteenth century, or they might be tapered and fluted. Neoclassical legs usually accompany a straight back and sides, while the turned-out sabre legs match splayed-out armrests. Back rests are usually completely straight, but the front rail is often richly carved. Footstools

follow the same principle as sofas. They have the same straight or turned pairs of legs and the same type of decoration on the front rail.

Inevitably, almost all sofas and footstools are painted and, since they have traditionally been the preserve of the more elegant household rather than the rural farmstead, pale Gustavian colours prevail, enlivened with the occasional splash of gilding. Most have loose upholstery, with cushions, small bolsters and squabs arrayed along the sides and seat. Some may have back cushions as a concession to comfort.

Some early sofas convert into beds – the original sofa-bed – providing useful extra accommodation for overnight guests. Others have storage drawers tucked discreetly away beneath the seat.

FAR LEFT *Beneath a pair of* kurbits *paintings stands a traditional pull-out cot bench, which would have provided an additional sleeping place for a guest. The blue and white checked upholstery complements an intricate blue and gold floral design along the dado line and border, while a pair of cushions, covered in a striped and floral print in matching colours, soften the hard, straight wooden back.*

LEFT *Another cot bench, this one with much more ornate and decorative carving on the back rest, stands between two windows in a dressing room. The floral print of the upholstery has also been used for the window blinds. The slightly splayed legs match the splayed line of the back rest.*

Chairs

The clever use of chairs, often placed against the walls of a room, is an important component of the traditional Swedish look. The impact of the Gustavian style is probably most evident in the design of chairs. The straight high-backed style of the seventeenth century and the sinuous curves of early eighteenth-century Rococo gave way at the end of the century to the straighter lines of Gustav III's Neoclassicism.

Perhaps the most imitated Swedish chair, and one that is now available as a piece of reproduction furniture, is the 'Medallion' chair seen in many of the rooms of the Courtiers' Wing at Gripsholm castle. This has a medallion back, an upholstered seat with rounded corners and turned legs. Often, there is carved decoration at the top of the back rest, at the centre of the front rail or in roundels at the top of the front legs.

Although a fondness for Rococo lingered on in a few curvaceous examples and in the shape of armrests, Gustavian taste was generally for straight or turned lines. One popular design has a wide, rectangular back rest consisting of simple, square-section uprights. The seat is either in plain wood, or upholstered for comfort. Another style boasts 'X' shaped back rests, while the nineteenth century brought lyre-shaped back rests and 'Klismos' chairs with curved backs and legs.

Corner chairs were also popular. They were often used at writing desks or evening tables and could be tucked away in a corner of the room when not in use.

Chairs in Swedish farmsteads saw less change than those in the homes of the wealthy and the middle classes. The ladderback chair was one of the staples of the Swedish peasant home, just as it was in country cottages all over Europe. With its plain wooden or rush seat, it was sturdy, practical and cheap.

As a fondness for rustic simplicity permeated the whole of Swedish society, the ladderback chair found its way into the homes of wealthier people, albeit in a more comfortable style. The Gripsholm chair is a case in point. So-called because many examples were used at Gripsholm, this has a wide back, an upholstered seat and upholstered armrests.

It is not difficult to find old chairs in similar shapes to those used in Swedish homes. Remember that Baroque chairs were often painted brown to imitate mahogany, walnut or rosewood, while in the Gustavian period most furniture was repainted in pale colours. Carl Larrson, on the other hand, sometimes painted antique chairs in bright peasant reds, blues and greens, enlivening their cool elegance with a vibrant colour scheme.

LEFT *A pair of Gripsholm chairs with red checked cushions combine comfort with tradition.*

RIGHT *These three chairs are, from top to bottom, a Medallion chair, a light wood chair with curved backrest and a Swedish interpretation of the type of corner chair commonly seen in England.*

OVERLEAF *The two elegant Neoclassical chairs in the centre are flanked by a Baroque example on the left and a Rococo chair on the right.*

PAINTED LETTERING

Decorative painted lettering adds a touch of Swedish wit and lightness to any piece of furniture. Originally, lettering was used to name the owner, to record a family event, or simply to label the contents of a drawer or cupboard.

MATERIALS AND EQUIPMENT

Matt water-based paints:
Cream
Red
Matt acrylic varnish

Decorator's brush
Artist's brushes
Tape measure or ruler
Tracing paper
Hard and soft pencils
Masking tape

LEFT *This antique chair has been personalized to make a unique present.*

RIGHT *Some of the many ways in which lettering can be used to playful and practical effect. In a country house north of Stockholm, the guest bedrooms have all been given numbers. Initials and a date have been painted on the doors of a wooden bureau in a warm reddish tone that matches the metal door furniture. A modern interpretation of apothecary-style lettering adds a traditional note to a chest of drawers.*

PREPARATION
1 Paint the furniture with the matt cream emulsion [latex]. If necessary prime beforehand with an acrylic primer.

MARKING OUT
2 Using the sample alphabet and numerals shown overleaf, trace the lettering you require onto a piece of tracing paper. Be sure to keep the spacing even between letters. The lettering can be 'punctuated' at the start and finish with the letter 'X' or a decorated cross.

3 Measure the area to be painted and, using a photocopier, reduce or enlarge the lettering to fit. Trace the photocopy onto a piece of tracing paper and retrace the outline on the reverse using a soft pencil. Do not use carbon paper as it leaves a dark, greasy line that is impossible to overpaint.

4 Measure and mark the centre point of the area to be painted and the centre point of the tracing paper design. Transfer the design to the piece of furniture, matching the centre points. It may be necessary to adjust the position of the tracing paper design before you trace it off in order to achieve the most pleasing effect. This is especially true on a chair back where the design may need adjusting from top to bottom.

PAINTING THE DESIGN
5 Using fine and medium artist's brushes, fill in the traced letters with red paint. When the paint is dry, varnish with two coats of matt acrylic varnish to seal and protect the surface if you wish.

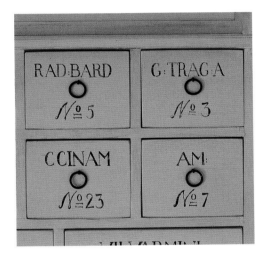

abcdefghij
klmnopqr
stuvwxyz

1234567890

Tiled Stoves

The stove is one of the most important features in a typically Swedish room, and traditional tiled versions are still used in many homes. The design of these stoves reached its apogee in the mid eighteenth century, when technical improvements revolutionized the lifestyle of the upper classes while providing designers with yet another outlet for their decorative ideas. One of the co-inventors of the new stove was Johan Cronstedt, a pupil of Court Architect Carl Hårleman, who decorated the interiors at Drottningholm. During the building of the manor of Claestorp, south-west of Stockholm, between 1754 and 1758, Cronstedt pondered over the problem of how to keep stoves warm for a long time. The very hard Swedish

winters meant that, even in grander homes, life revolved around only a few rooms at a time because of the difficulty of heating them. Cronstedt experimented with stoves designed to force the smoke from the fire up and down through a series of pipes and ducts set in heat-retaining bricks before it was allowed to pass out through the chimney. Tiled exteriors also helped to retain and reflect heat. These new stoves were vastly more efficient than the old ones had been and they remained warm for hours after the fire had gone out. Now furniture could be moved out of the huddle surrounding an open fireplace and arranged elegantly against the wall instead.

Although open stoves, with the fire box

BELOW, FROM LEFT TO RIGHT *These three examples of Swedish stoves show the different kinds of design used on their decorative tiles. The formal, architectural lines of a classical design match the painted wall panels in a period room. The gleaming doors of the fire box add a luxurious touch. A repeated blue and white motif has been used for this antique stove in a modernized cottage. When polychrome stoves became the fashion, vibrant green was one of the most popular colours.*

RIGHT *Details of tiles used as repeating motifs on four early stoves. A special firing process was developed to ensure that the background glaze remained white and bright even after many years of exposure to high temperatures.*

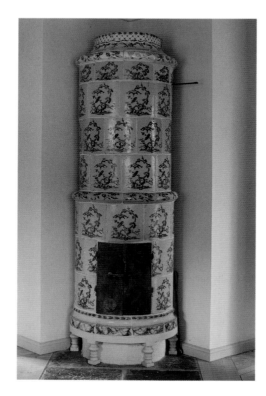

at eye level, remained a feature of almost every farmhouse during the course of the eighteenth century, tiled stoves made their appearance in manor houses and *stugor* throughout the country, as the wealthy installed them in place of open fireplaces. Many of those in grander houses were made between 1758 and 1788 at the Marieberg faience and porcelain factory, which was partly owned by Gustav III's finance minister Count Liljencrantz. The decorations on these stoves were often very elaborate and included family crests, brightly coloured flowers and Chinese-inspired motifs on the tiles. In some examples the taste for Classicism is evident, with the tops of the stoves shaped to resemble columns and ornamented with elaborate swags and urns or with bows and leaves.

On occasion, the Gustavian taste for symmetry led to a stove being copied in wood to make a cupboard which was then placed on the opposite side of the room from the real stove. The copy, with painted tile decoration, was hardly distinguishable from the real thing. Nowadays, however, the tiles of the stoves retain their crisp whiteness, while the painted wood of the copy has usually yellowed with age.

In the first decade of the nineteenth century the fashion changed. Repeating motifs and multi-coloured designs were replaced by monochrome tiles and the wooden or iron legs which held the stove above the floor gave way to unglazed ceramic plinths which could be painted to resemble stone. Fine examples of both styles can be seen at Carl Larsson's house.

In a shop in Saltsjöbaden, outside Stockholm, a designer has managed to create a happy mix of reproduction furniture. The stove on the right is actually a painted wooden cupboard, made to look like an old stove. This practice takes its inspiration from period interiors, where a fake stove was sometimes placed on the opposite side of a room from a real one to achieve a symmetrical look. There is no reason why this clever idea should not be used to provide extra storage in any room where a real stove is not practicable. The detail of work in progress shows how the tile design is pencilled onto the cupboard before being painted.

Storage

Given the Swedish fondness for lack of clutter, storage in the form of cupboards and chests of drawers is important in any design scheme. These pieces are often very decorative items and come in a variety of forms. In a Swedish home today one might find old family heirlooms, lovingly preserved and restored, or examples of new reproduction cupboards and chests of drawers painted in appropriately Gustavian style.

Low cupboards or sideboards as well as dressers are common in the dining room, where they are used to store silver and table linen. Set against a wall or beneath a window they look good adorned with nothing more than a centrally placed bowl of flowers or a piece of blue and white porcelain flanked by a pair of candlesticks. The larger pieces can be multi-functional. A pull-down flap, for example, will convert a dresser into a bureau.

Chests of drawers and combinations of drawers with cupboards are as much at home in bedrooms as they are in living or dining rooms. In the bedroom, as well as storing clothes and bed linen, they can be made to double up as a dressing table simply by leaning a mirror on top against the wall. Larger cupboards or *armoires* provide hanging space with storage above for blankets and sheets.

Decoration of these pieces of furniture varies. The attempt to create a classical column effect can determine the shape of an entire piece, but other carving may be added simply as embellishment – the pilasters and lyres carved on the front of one sideboard or the lozenges on door

LEFT *In the dressing room of an old country house, a painted chest of drawers has been used to hold clothes for generations. Additional storage space is hidden behind the doors of the boarded wall cupboards, cleverly painted with a frieze and incorporating a false dado to match the rest of the room.*

BELOW *A painted cupboard dating from 1862 is decorated with rustic trellised panels, surrounded by false wood grain. On top, a crown of buttercups has been left to dry.*

and drawer fronts of another. Reeding and the lozenge are popular forms of ornament. On some simple chests of drawers, lozenge-shaped escutcheons are the only embellishment.

Painting is, of course, another form of decoration for this and other types of furniture. Rustic pieces are traditionally painted in the darker greens, blues and reds and often with complex *kurbits*-style designs. Stencilling on chests of drawers and cupboards also suits the rustic look. Red and yellow ochre stencilled over a dark green base is a popular combination that can easily be copied.

Marbling is found both on country pieces, where the effect might be fanciful, and on more elegant chests and cupboards. It is not a difficult technique to copy, and the finished results are well worth the effort (see pages 92-3). Marbled wood may be easier to live with than real marble, which can look cold and hard.

More elegant Gustavian pieces are painted in lighter colours – white, creamy yellow, soft green and pearl grey – as one would expect. Original pieces have a gently faded look that can easily be copied onto painted junk-shop finds. Some judicious rubbing-back of new paint can achieve the required effect, but for the correct look, it is important to ensure that the furniture you choose to paint shares the same spare, clean lines of the Gustavian originals.

Another paint effect much used on cupboards is spattering, often confined to the interior of the doors to add an element of surprise. This look is easy to achieve and can be carried out in light Gustavian colours, or in earthy, rustic colours for a more rural feel (see pages 88-9).

ABOVE LEFT *A nineteenth-century white-painted corner cupboard is used to store china and glass in a country house. In many homes, a cupboard like this would have been mirrored by another in the adjoining corner of the room to create a symmetrical effect.*

ABOVE RIGHT *This modern reproduction cupboard is two separate pieces. Each of the drawers in the lower section has been decorated with a picture of a different Swedish lighthouse.*

LEFT *A modern interpretation of the traditional Swedish sideboard with lots of small drawers and three cupboards. The diamond-shaped panels are carved in the old manner.*

RIGHT *Open shelving is used to great effect in the dining area of a very old country parstuga. The bright cornflower blue of the low-beamed ceiling is carried down to the shelves where it provides a perfect backdrop for the display of antique crockery.*

A FLORAL MOTIF FOR FURNITURE

This garland of leaves and buds was taken from the side panel of a Swedish cupboard painted in reds and greens on a background of different greys. The side panel design was modified to make a border for the cupboard's cornice and was also used as the basis for the design on the door. It could easily be adapted for use on a chair or table.

MATERIALS AND EQUIPMENT

Matt water-based paints:
Two shades of green
Two shades of red
Matt acrylic varnish

Artist's brushes
Tape measure or ruler
Straightedge
Spirit level
Soft pencil

ABOVE AND ABOVE LEFT *Painted cupboards have long been a common sight in Swedish rural homes, and stylized flowers were often used as decorative motifs. In an antique corner cupboard at Skansen Museum they form an all-over pattern, but in the cupboard which provided the inspiration for this project, the flowers are part of a leafy border.*

MARKING OUT THE DESIGN

1 Measurements for the design on a 45cm/18in panel are given here. To adapt it for a smaller or larger piece, adjust the measurements but keep the proportions roughly the same.

Measure across the top and bottom of the panel and mark the centre points. Using a soft pencil and a straightedge join these points to mark the vertical centre of the design. Make a pencil mark on the line 80mm/3in from the bottom of the panel. Measure and mark a second point 10cm/4in up from the first, then mark a third point 25mm/1in from the second, a fourth 10cm/4in from the third, a fifth 25mm/1in from the fourth and so on, ending approximately 13cm/5in from the top of the panel. Using a soft pencil draw pairs of upward-curving leaves in the 10cm/4in gaps **(a)**. Add a single extra leaf to the top pair of leaves. Do not worry if the leaves vary in size and design as this will add to their charm.

PAINTING THE LEAVES

2 Using a medium artist's brush, fill in the leaves with the lighter green paint **(b)** and leave to dry. When the paint is completely dry, use a pencil to draw the sprays of small leaves sprouting from one pair of large leaves in each group **(c)**.

3 Using a fine artist's brush, paint the sprays of small leaves with the lighter green paint **(d)**. Leave to dry.

PAINTING THE SECOND COLOUR

4 Fill the remaining spaces along the original pencil line with three joined circles – the flower buds – pencilled in freehand. A single circle sits on top of a pair of circles forming a rough downward-pointing triangle. Using a medium artist's brush, paint them in the paler red and leave to dry. When the flower buds have dried, use the fine artist's brush and the darker red to outline them with shading **(e)**. Leave to dry.

5 When the darker red has dried, use a fine artist's brush and the darker green paint to outline the larger leaves and add veins. Use the same brush and colour to paint the calyx of each group of flower buds **(f)**.

6 To achieve the antique distressed look of the cupboard shown here, mix together a little of the two shades of green paint used in the project, dilute with the same amount of water and use this mixture to spatter the finished work (see pages 88-9). Once this is dry, apply two coats of matt acrylic varnish to seal and protect the surface if you wish.

a
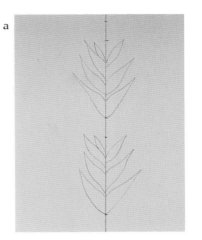

b
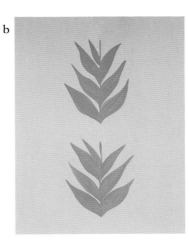

c

d

e

f

A SPATTERED CUPBOARD

Spatter painting was traditionally carried out using birch twigs to flick paint onto the surface, but a paintbrush works just as well. Applied to the inside of a cupboard door, spattering adds a subtle element of surprise.

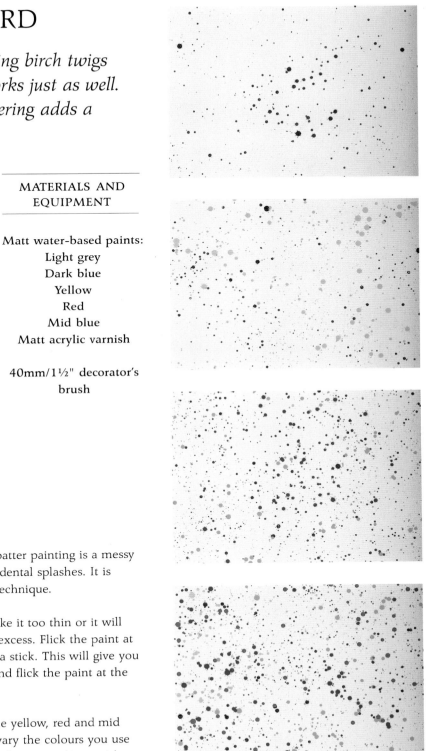

MATERIALS AND EQUIPMENT

Matt water-based paints:
Light grey
Dark blue
Yellow
Red
Mid blue
Matt acrylic varnish

40mm/1½" decorator's brush

1 Prime your piece of furniture with the light grey water-based paint. Spatter painting is a messy technique, so make sure the surrounding area is well protected from accidental splashes. It is advisable to practise first on paper to make sure you have mastered the technique.

2 Slightly dilute the paint so that it will fly off the brush, but do not make it too thin or it will run. Dip the tip of the brush into the dark blue paint and shake off any excess. Flick the paint at the surface by hitting the stock of the loaded paintbrush sharply against a stick. This will give you a series of small dots of colour. For larger dots, dispense with the stick and flick the paint at the surface using a brisk motion of the wrist.

3 Wait for the first spatter coat to dry and repeat the procedure using the yellow, red and mid blue paint, gradually building up to the final effect. You can, of course, vary the colours you use to suit your decorative scheme. When all coats are dry, apply two coats of matt acrylic varnish.

Tables

Swedes have their large dining tables and practical pine kitchen tables like anyone else, but where they have always excelled is in the use of small side tables and versatile, foldaway tables. The same piece of furniture can be used to hold drinks in a living room, as a desk, as a kitchen table, as a bedside table, or as a dressing table. In homes with high bench-like sofas, which oblige you to sit upright, it is far more comfortable to use a taller folding table in front of the sofa than a low coffee table. The surface will then be the right height for writing, reading or eating. When the task is complete, the table can be folded away and put back against a wall, where it will take up less room.

The dropleaf table, seen in France and England from the 1730s onwards, was also adopted by the Swedes. Extended fully, it makes a fine dining table; when half closed and set beside a window, it can be used as a desk. To maximize space, both leaves can be lowered and the narrow central section that remains can be set beside a sofa, or used as a sideboard.

As well as the dropleaf style, there are simple, rectangular tables with Rococo cabriole legs. Cabriole, tapered, or turned and reeded legs support half-round tables, writing tables or kitchen work tables.

Occasional tables for drinks may have simple pedestal bases and tops marbled to look like stone, or plain ones with carved 'pie-crust' edges. Some little tea tables have practical faience trays inserted on the top. These tables were probably once used with a jug and basin as wash-stands, the tray catching water spilt during ablutions.

ABOVE *Four very different styles demonstrate the variety of occasional tables found in Swedish homes. A plain, straight-legged table with a boarded top has been transformed into a unique piece by marbling, though the slightly primitive result suggests that the painter had never seen true marble. An antique faience tray has been made into a table with the addition of a specially commissioned base. The long low table and the taller tripod table rely on the simplicity of the painted wood for their impact.*

RIGHT *This typical Swedish furniture layout shows a tea table with cabriole legs set in front of an antique cot sofa. In smaller Swedish homes, meals were traditionally eaten while sitting on the sofa, making a high table a necessity. The unusual pull-out extensions at each end of the table have here been used to hold candlesticks, but could also provide an additional surface area for a variety of other purposes, to hold an extra teacup or plate perhaps.*

A MARBLED TABLE

*Lacking examples of marble to copy, Swedish decorators often produced marbling that was
no more than an approximation of the original material, but which created a charming fantasy effect.
The lively marbling on this tilt-top table is easy to achieve and could be adapted for other surfaces,
such as doors or fireplaces. Acrylic varnish has been used to add depth and translucency,
and to give the surface a smooth, glossy finish.*

MATERIALS AND EQUIPMENT

Matt water-based paints:
Grey-green and red-brown
Matt acrylic glaze tinted dark green
with artist's acrylic paint
Acrylic scumble glaze tinted light green
with artist's acrylic paint
Satin finish acrylic varnish

Decorator's and artist's brushes
Flogging brush or old wallpaper brush
Chalk

PREPARATION

1 Paint the table top with the grey-green paint and the base with the red-brown paint **(a)** using a 50mm/2in decorator's brush. If necessary prime beforehand with an acrylic primer.

MARKING OUT

2 Using the chalk, cover the table top with the outlines of large flat bubble shapes interspersed with smaller ones **(b)**.

PAINTING

3 Using a 12mm/½in artist's brush and the dark green acrylic glaze, loosely paint over the chalked outlines **(c)**. Allow to dry.

4 Use a decorator's brush to apply the tinted scumble glaze to the table top. While the scumble glaze is still wet, use the dry flogging brush – a brush with long bristles that splay out slightly at their tips to give a loosely brushed effect – or an old wallpaper brush, to drag it off, leaving the impression of the bristles in the glaze **(d)**. Work in the direction of the wood grain. Allow to dry, then apply two coats of satin finish water- and heat-resistant acrylic varnish to seal and protect the entire table.

a

b

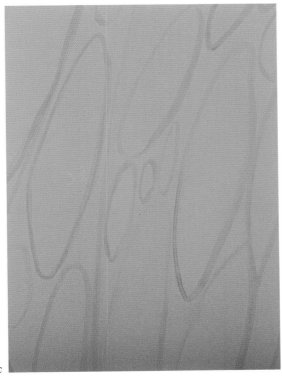

c

d

Beds

In traditional country homes beds were often tucked away in closets or alcoves, behind either curtains or doors. This saved space in what was often the main room, used for cooking, eating and sleeping by the whole family. Another space-saving trick in rural farmhouses and peasant cottages was to set a bed lengthwise against a wall and build a cupboard in place of the footboard, thus providing sleeping and storage accommodation in a single fitment. A scheme of this sort was used for Karin Larsson's bed at Lilla Hyttnäs (see pages 18-19). Elsewhere in the Larssons' house, the children slept in bunk beds with doors which could be shut like cupboards. Drawers beneath a bed, or a small sofa at the foot as a step-up were also common in Swedish houses.

Many of these rural ideas worked their way into other strands of society and remain a feature of Swedish style today.

In the Courtiers' Wing at Gripsholm Castle, all the beds are placed in alcoves that can be screened from view by a curtain. The design of some beds from the time of Gustav III is indicative of the cramped living conditions of the day. With their delicately carved head- and footboards, and turned legs, they are extendable lengthways. When not in use during the day the footboard can be pushed towards the headboard thus reducing the bed to half its normal length and saving space. More common is the bench bed, which pulls out sideways to make a double bed and has extra storage space in the drawers beneath.

Much of the attractiveness of the Swedish-style bedroom lies in the way the bed is decorated with bedhangings, which now serve an aesthetic rather than a practical purpose. Hung from poles or coronas above the centre of the bed, simple muslin or printed calico is draped over the head and feet to give a cosy, tent-like feel. Alternatively, the fabric can be hung from a semi-circular corona above the bedhead (see page 105).

LEFT *On this free-standing version of a Louis XVI bed a wooden frame is topped with a small circular corona and draped with white muslin. A clever carpenter could copy this idea, which does not need any ceiling or wall-mounted fittings.*

RIGHT *A similar but much simpler effect is achieved by extending a pole from the wall above the bed and hanging white muslin drapes over it to fall over the ends of the bed.*

FABRICS

LOOK AT THE USE of fabrics in any contemporary Swedish interior and you will immediately see the influence of the eighteenth-century Gustavian style. The overall effect is minimalist. Upholstery, window treatments and bedding are almost always cotton or linen. Patterns are used sparingly and usually take the form of woven checks and stripes or delicate floral prints. The predominant colours are white, blue, pale green, pale yellow, red and ecru, the colour of unbleached linen, with occasional touches of brown ochre or bottle green. You rarely see a fabric with more than one or two colours against a white or ecru background. The resulting look is all the more powerful because each fabric is allowed to speak for itself; it is not lost in a riot of colour but harmonizes gently with its neighbour. Neither is it overlaid with elaborate trimmings that would detract from the inherent simplicity of the textile.

Fashions come and go, as they have done in the two hundred years since Gustav III. Like other Europeans, the Swedes succumbed to the mid nineteenth-century taste for heavy velvet and brocade upholstery and for elaborate curtains with pelmets, tails and swags at their windows. But their love of simplicity inevitably brought them back to the pared-down Gustavian look that is epitomized so

The fabrics chosen for this drawing room give a real lift and lightness to the otherwise formal decor. On the corner settee, a floral cotton print covers both the upholstered seat and the separate scatter cushions, while the toning stripes on the chairs and the muslin swag over the window complete the traditional look.

beautifully in the Courtiers' Wing at Gripsholm Castle. Here, in rooms decorated in the 1780s, fabrics are used with such a light touch and they are so practical – always hardwearing, washable cottons or linens in simple designs – that it is not surprising that they appeal to the modern eye and to modern taste. Easy to copy and easy to live with, the Gripsholm fabrics adapt readily to urban living throughout the world or to the traditional country-house look. They sit equally well with antique furniture or with the classic designs of the twentieth century.

During Gustav III's reign, State rooms and the private apartments of the royal family were decorated with the taffeta, brocaded silk and satins then fashionable at the French court. For those even slightly lower down the social scale, however, plain or checked native linen or delicate one-colour floral cotton prints offered a synthesis of French sophistication and Swedish resourcefulness.

The Swedes had a thriving textile industry of their own in the eighteenth century, but they were always aware of the economic necessity to reduce the level of imported raw materials. Flax for the making of linen was one commodity of which there was an ample supply, so linen cloth was universally used. Cotton and silk, on the other hand, had to be imported and so remained the preserve of the wealthy. The northern province of Hälsingland was the centre of the Swedish linen industry. In the days before the technique of printing on fabric was perfected, any pattern had to be woven into the cloth. The simplest possible designs were therefore stripes or checks in one or two colours.

Linen damask required a more sophisticated method of weaving. The Flor Manufaktori, established around 1700, was the first factory in Sweden to produce it. Within fifty years the Swedish State had begun actively to pursue a policy of encouraging the textile industry and in 1753, with State help, a cambric and fine linen mill was founded at Vadstena. Here, with the assistance of foreign specialists, linen production was developed on a large scale from cultivation of the flax to dressing and the spinning, and in the 1770s Vadstena too started weaving its own linen damask using patterns based on models from abroad. So successful was the newly developing linen industry that its products were chosen to form part of the original decor at Gripsholm, where chairs were covered in a pale green linen weave.

Wool was another native product. During the Baroque period it occupied a social position somewhere between silk and linen. There were always lots of small-scale textile producers who used wool of Swedish origin, but in the eighteenth century the State made determined efforts to develop better quality wool for the manufacturers. The extent to which imports dominated the Swedish wool market can be seen in the collection assembled in the mid eighteenth century by Anders Berch, first professor of economics at Uppsala University, as a teaching tool for his students. Of 1,118 samples of woollen and worsted cloths, 744 came from England. Interestingly, most of the printed textiles in the collection were on woollen cloth.

In the eighteenth century, printed cottons imported from France were the

height of fashion – as indeed was anything French – but the Swedes did print their own cottons too, for instance at the calico-printing works at Sickla near Stockholm, founded in 1729. They also had a small cotton industry – a weaving mill was established at Sickla in 1742 to make the white calico for printing – but most cotton fabrics came from India via the Swedish East India Company.

Silks were largely imported from China, Persia, Italy, France and England. The Swedish State encouraged silkworm production on a small scale in the mid eighteenth century, and in 1762 the area around Stockholm boasted forty-one silk mills, but silks were used only in the very richest homes. Native linen woven in stripes and checks or simple cotton prints remained closer to the hearts and purses of the Swedes. Even in one of the regal bedrooms at Gripsholm where imported painted Chinese silk taffeta graced the walls, the curtains were made of checked silk. It is as though the decorators yearned for the simplicity of a peasant textile.

In addition to plain weaves, the ancient technique of *rya* or rug-weaving was widely used for making quilts and small wallhangings. This involved knotting yarn, animal hair or pieces of rag around two or more warp threads of a linen, cotton, hemp or coir backing. Originally *rya* was used with the pile facing downwards for warmth: the decoration was then concentrated in the weave of the backing material and the pile was set close together to cover the whole of the backing material. Only at the end of the 1600s did people start to turn the *rya* pile side up and use it for more ornamental effect, arranging the pile in a pattern.

LEFT *Keeping to the red and green of the painted linen wall panel above the bed, this country style coverlet has been made in the traditional* rya *technique, with rich woollen patterns added to hand loomed linen.*

BELOW *This bedspread shows a variation on the* rya *technique in which strips of fabric are knotted into the linen to form the patterned decoration. The pillowslips and valance are edged in red cross–stitch embroidery.*

OVERLEAF *A selection of typical Swedish woven and printed fabrics gives a guide to the sort of patterns to look for. They are rarely multicoloured and often incorporate some sort of stripe. Here they are seen on a range of reproduction Swedish chairs which are readily available today.*

Contrasting fabrics are central to the overall effect in this recently decorated guest bedroom in a house north of Stockholm. The canopied day bed is upholstered in a delicate French floral print, while the bedspread is a complementary floral cotton, as is the inside of the tester, or canopy. The use of French fabric is entirely appropriate to this modern interpretation of the Gustavian style, since printed cottons imported from France were highly fashionable in eighteenth-century Sweden.

The white chair, the footstool, the bed and the table provide a perfect foil for the red and blue of the textiles, while the hand-loomed cotton carpet further enhances the fresh effect. Swathes of pure white muslin are used for bedhangings and to soften the windows. The muslin swag is held in place with little rosettes and the curtains are secured by a pair of metal tie-backs. As a final inspired detail, a silk embroidered picture is suspended from the cornice with a blue and white taffeta ribbon and bow.

Upholstery

The most important element of Swedish-style upholstery is its simplicity, which makes it easy and inexpensive to copy. As a starting point for the look you will need to find chairs or sofas with an eighteenth-century Neoclassical feel – clean lines, minimal carved detail and the wood painted white or grey with a distressed finish. Large, squashy sofas, deep armchairs and mahogany chairs in the English country-house style are definitely unsuitable.

Swedish chair seats are squarish or rounded and tight-covered, while the backrest is occasionally upholstered but more often left plain. Wooden arms, if the chair has them, are either plain or have padded elbow rests. Sofas are similarly austere. They often have carved wooden backrests, upholstery along the back usually being restricted to long squabs laid on boards and covered in the same fabric as the seat. To provide additional comfort and to soften the line there may be a small bolster cushion at each end. The long bench seats in peasant homes frequently had long cushions specially made for them, but there is no evidence that scatter cushions were traditionally used in Swedish homes.

RIGHT *The printed green, red and white cotton fabric on this semi-upholstered chair stands out as the only patterned note in a room of plain surfaces. The padded elbow rests, seat pad and upholstered loose back cushion make the chair as comfortable to sit in as it is stylish to look at.*

The fabrics to complement this austerity must be unfussy too, otherwise the chairs and sofas would be overwhelmed. A plain linen weave is a suitable choice, in pale blue, pale grey, pale green, pale yellow or unbleached linen. If you want to add more colour, do so sparingly, remembering the limited palette used in Gustavian times. Keep to woven cottons or linens in two-tone checks or stripes, or, if you want to add pattern, take a simple two-tone floral design or one of the attractive prints or weaves that combine stripes with elegant leaves or flowers twining the length of the stripes. There are also some attractive woven cottons with embroidered flower motifs on top of the weave, which will produce a suitably quiet, Neoclassical look. Toile de Jouy, with its idyllic pastoral or oriental scenes in muted two-tone colours offers further alternative which would have been available to eighteenth-

century Swedes, who had a particular affection for printed fabrics from France.

If you are covering several different pieces of furniture in different fabrics, be sure that the fabrics complement each other. Select your colours from the pale Gustavian palette and ensure that they tone, since any sharp contrasts would add a jarring note. Patterns should be of a similar size and scale so that large, bold designs do not swamp smaller, less obvious ones. Velvets or brocades would look entirely out of keeping, so restrict yourself to cotton or linen.

Tight-covered seats are the most common but you might like to ring the changes, as people often do in Sweden, by using loose covers in summer. At one time loose calico or linen covers protected the very expensive fitted upholstery from dust and direct sunlight, in grand eighteenth-century houses, for example, when a room was not in use, and in

summer houses that were shut up in winter. Made in striped or checked linen, simple covers of this kind could either be plain or have a frill around the edge. They often had a tape folded over the edges of the main material which was extended at the vents to provide ribbon ties to attach it to the chair. This idea can be copied today, or fabric-covered velcro tabs used instead.

BELOW *This pair of benches illustrates the importance of selecting the right upholstery fabrics for different types of furniture. For a formal Gustavian bench, on which some of the carved detail has been picked out in sumptuous gold leaf, the seat has been upholstered in a striped satined cotton, its straight lines continuing the vertical bars of the back. The only concession to comfort comes in the form of two bolsters. A more rustic hall bench, beautifully carved and painted in faded grey, is upholstered in a hardwearing checked linen.*

LEFT *In the hallway of an old farmhouse the seat of a painted wooden armchair has been given a loose cover in plain white linen, shaped to fit the contours of the seat and tied in place. The clean lines of the cover perfectly complement the rectangular austerity of the antique linen press.*

ABOVE AND RIGHT *A less formal look has been achieved for the painted hard-backed chairs in this kitchen by using loose cotton covers with a gathered frill. Against the cream, yellow and ochre of walls and floors, the blue and white stripe on the chairs provides a cheerful contrast. The loose cover conceals and protects an upholstered seat covered in closely woven blue and white checked material. Typically Swedish in its effect, the fabric for the cover is carefully tailored to fit the shape of the seat and attached with velcro tabs to the back of the chair so that it is easy to remove for laundering. For wooden-seated chairs, the usual practice is to add a touch of comfort by taking a flat squab cushion the same size as the chair base and making a frilled cover for it. The whole cushion can then be tied to the chair back in the same way.*

Bed Treatments

The use of very simple fabrics to dress up a bed is one of the hallmarks of the Gustavian look which appears romantic and friendly to twentieth-century eyes. It is equally adaptable to a traditional home or to a modern but not too minimalist setting. It is also easy to copy and need not cost a fortune. The fabrics to choose are inexpensive muslins and two-tone cottons either printed in floral patterns or woven in stripes and checks. Colours should be limited to the Gustavian palette – pale yellow, pale blue, pale green or red against a background of white or unbleached linen.

Historically, beds were often set in shallow alcoves, dressed with prettily printed calico curtains and pelmets. The original purpose of bedhangings was to protect the occupant of the bed from cold and draughts. Gradually, as more efficient stoves were introduced, the overall warmth of the room improved and the bedhangings became less practical and more decorative. Although the hangings of the Gripsholm beds are copies in simpler fabrics of the silk and brocade in the royal apartments, bedhangings even in wealthy eighteenth-century homes would frequently be made from imported worsteds or locally produced and woven linen. Gustav III's courtiers would not have been surprised to see the simple fabrics used in the decoration of the rooms they were to inhabit. In fact, by eighteenth-century European standards, these courtiers' rooms were lavish.

To copy this style, it is not necessary to have a bed in an alcove. A tented effect can easily be achieved by suspending

ABOVE *In this guest room a cot bed with a wooden frame is crowned with a circular corona and draped with white muslin in a checked weave to create an appearance of understated luxury. A narrow frill softens the vertical edges of the fabric. The textured diamond pattern woven into the bed cover, a simple throw-over in a heavier cotton, provides a slight variation on the squares in the muslin. Keeping both the coverlet and the muslin drapes short prevents the overall effect from becoming too solid and heavy, while the blue and white stripe in the chair cover makes a pleasing contrast.*

RIGHT *The fabrics used in this twin-bedded guest room have been carefully selected to fall within a limited range of blues against a background of white. The floral stripe of the French cotton used for the quilted bedcovers and padded headboards is echoed in the striped muslin drapes hung from the windows and the semicircular canopies. At the end of each bed stands a finely carved wooden stool with a tied-on loose cover in pale grey-blue checks protecting the upholstered seat. With walls, furniture, rug and paintwork all in a similar shade, this room offers both visual tranquillity and a sense of relaxed comfort.*

muslin drapes from a corona over the bed or simply from a length of pole attached to the wall. If the foot of the bed faces into the room, the drapes can also hang from a small half-tester, either bought ready-made or cut to shape from wooden moulding, painted and screwed to the ceiling. Alternatively, stand the bed with its long side against the wall in the style of a daybed – a form of furniture very popular in eighteenth-century Sweden – and suspend the hangings above the centre of the bed's long side. Checks, stripes and toile de Jouy-type textiles offer striking and effective alternatives to muslin drapes, but be sure not to choose a stiff fabric or it will not hang well.

An attractively carved or moulded headboard and footboard – painted white or pale grey – may be upholstered in cotton or linen too. For an authentic Gustavian look, use the same or a matching fabric for any additional chairs in the room.

When choosing fabrics for Swedish-style bedhangings, it pays to remember that they should, on the whole, echo rather than contrast with other furnishings and paint treatments in the room. Do not be tempted to overdo the frills or flounces. The simpler the better. The same is true for the bedding. The courtiers at Gripsholm would originally have slept on down mattresses, often with a second down mattress on top covered with striped, quilted or embroidered cotton. The Swedish preference is for simple cotton duvet covers in pale colours, or in soft checks or stripes with matching pillowslips in the lighter colour. The effect you should be looking to achieve is one of simple and unadorned harmony.

Window Treatments

With their long, dark winters, the Swedes wish to allow as much light as possible into their rooms. Most older homes are double-glazed and all new houses are now constructed with triple glazing, so there is no need for heavy curtains to keep out the cold. Even before the days of central heating, heavy log walls in rural homes provided good insulation, absorbing heat from the large open fireplace and reflecting it back into the room.

One of the chief delights of Swedish window treatments is their simplicity. The effect of the sun filtering through a plain white muslin curtain has a pure beauty which is particularly attractive and easy to achieve without spending large sums of money on exotic and expensive fabrics.

The simplest muslin swag with short tails, perhaps caught into a rosette at each corner and simply draped above a window, is all you need to create a Swedish window treatment instantly. One simple idea which might be seen as the embodiment of Swedish style is very easy to copy. For this you make a large single swag from a plain, white cotton sheet. Catch it back at each side at the top of the window with an elastic band and draw

LEFT *A plain cotton curtain suspended by fabric loops on a simple string lets in light from the top part of the window yet still affords some privacy.*

RIGHT *Many windows in Sweden are draped in some manner with cotton muslin. These four examples show a variety of the weaves and patterns to look for.*

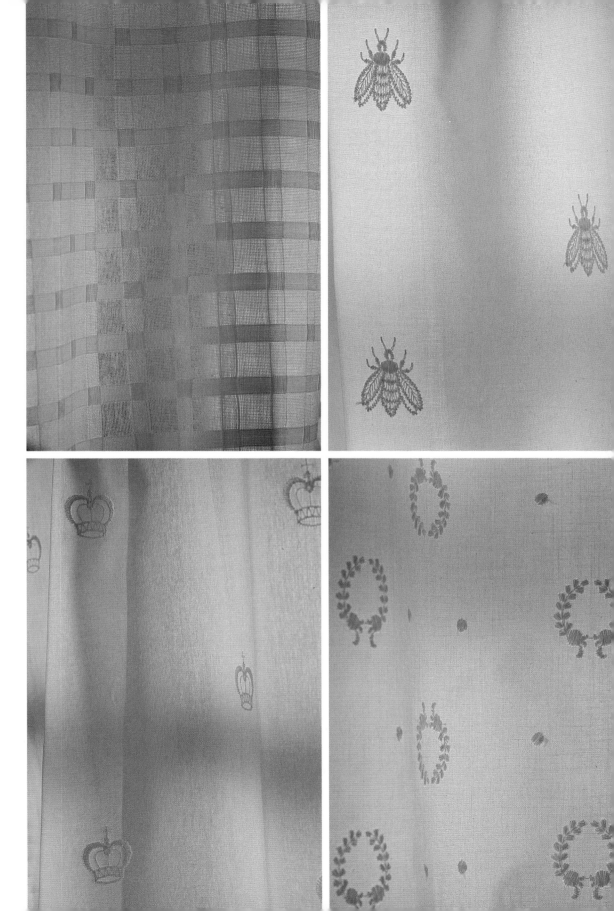

ABOVE *In a summer pavilion outside Stockholm, all the windows have a woven patterned muslin swag, held up with charming period metal swag holders in the form of bunches of grapes.*

RIGHT *This house in London decorated by its Swedish owner has unlined, printed cotton, floor-length curtains. The fabric is gathered onto plain brass rods and held back with acanthus leaf-shaped curtain bosses. Cushions covered in antique toile de Jouy are placed on the window seats.*

FAR RIGHT *Three examples of different ways to keep curtains open during the day. At the top, a woven cotton muslin curtain in a bedroom is held in place with a boss covered in check fabric. This is called a cloak pin, as it was originally used for hanging up cloaks or coats. The middle picture shows a curved brass arm holding back a bright gingham curtain in a country kitchen. At the bottom, an antique metal swag bracket depicting grapes and leaves catches up a length of draped white muslin with a woven pattern in a very stylish manner.*

the sheet through to create a rosette. Fix the sheet to the top of the window frame with hooks, nails or screws. The ends then hang down on either side of the window to give a simple and pleasing line.

Nowadays you may find Swedish curtains of all lengths. Some reach to the floor, some only to the windowsill, while others are nothing more than a pelmet or valance of crunchy white crochet across the top of the window frame, or a small muslin swag above it. Alternatively, for a truly rustic look, a plain white cotton half-curtain may be suspended by self-fabric ties from a curtain wire halfway down the window.

The one element all these ideas have in common is their simplicity. You need use nothing more than a piece of inexpensive white muslin or cotton to achieve the same look. Add some narrow crochet edging to the muslin if you find it a bit bare without. If you can afford it, choose a more expensive muslin with a self-pattern of stripes, bees, crowns or wreaths, all designs in keeping with the cool elegance of Swedish Neoclassicism and the slightly later Empire style.

Curtain tie-backs are equally simple. Muslin curtains are loosely gathered and held by a small leather thong or a rubber band. Another excellent choice is to hang the muslin over a white metal bracket that is invisible when in use. If you do wish to use a more elaborate device, choose one that is derived from Neoclassical motifs as a reminder of the effect on Gustavian style of the discoveries at Pompeii and Herculaneum. There are many brass or gilded tie-backs available in the form of rosettes or wreaths, or you can use plain metal bands.

A MUSLIN SWAG

The fluid muslin swag, seen adorning windows throughout Sweden, is extremely simple to assemble. The traditional method involves very little sewing, and uses elastic bands or string to secure the knots.

MATERIALS AND EQUIPMENT

Muslin
Tape measure
Two large nails
Two strong elastic bands
or thin string
Pins

MEASURING THE MUSLIN

1 You will need a rectangle of muslin at least 2m/6ft 6in longer than the width of your window and 1m/3ft 3in wide. Most European patterned muslins are woven in 3m/10ft widths, and used widthways across the window, but if the muslin is narrower, or your window is particularly wide, it is best to use the fabric lengthways and buy a longer length. If the muslin is very fine, or you want to make a long swag, you will need to use more fabric.

First machine-sew a 12mm/ ½in hem around the edges; lay the muslin flat, find the middle, and working from there outwards mark a point half the width of the window on either side. This marks the inner edge of the knots.

CREATING THE KNOT

2 Gather up about 30cm/ 12in of fabric from beyond this point and scrunch it into a knot (a). Secure it either with an elastic band or some thin string. Repeat for the other side. This will leave two equal lengths either side for the tails that hang down.

HANGING THE SWAG

3 After hammering two long nails into the top corners of the window frame, first slip one knot onto a nail. Now stretch the swag across the top of the window, and attach the other knot to the other nail. Keeping the top of the fabric taut, ease the lower edge of the material through the elastic band or string so that it falls in even, hanging folds. You might need some pins to keep the top taut, and it may take several attempts to achieve the required effect. Those who use the elastic bands method in Sweden say that when the sun wears out the bands and they snap, it is time for the swags to be washed and rehung.

ROSETTES

If you prefer formal rosettes to knots at the corners of the swags these can be made independently and pinned on once the swag is hung at the window (b). You will need to allow an extra 75cm/30in length of fabric for each rosette. Cut two circles of muslin approximately 75cm/ 30in in diameter. Use a needle and cotton to sew running stitch around the circumference, 20mm/¾in from the edge, and pull the thread tight to scrunch the fabric into a rosette. Secure the folds with some hidden stitches on the back of the rosette.

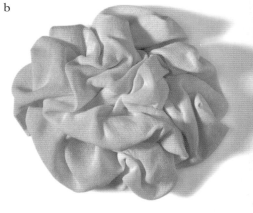

SWAG HOLDERS

An alternative method of hanging swags is to use special metal swag holders (c). These are attached to the wall, and the fabric is eased through them. You can bunch up the muslin to make a knot, or attach a rosette to hide the swag holder.

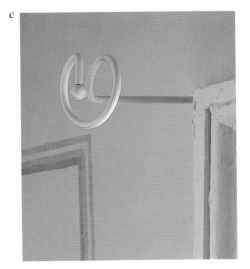

Roller blinds have long been popular in Sweden, even in rather grand settings where they were often used to prevent the fading of precious furniture, painted wallhangings and fabrics. They are frequently seen in conjunction with muslin swags. While some rely on a spring mechanism at the top, in most cases the form of construction is based on a simple system of glass hoops and strings which draw the blind up from the bottom. This is an easy system for an inexperienced home decorator to copy. For best effect, choose either a plain linen or cotton, or a weave of stripes or checks on a white or ecru background. The contrast colour can be pale yellow, pale green, pale blue, grey, red or bottle green. During the day blinds may be left half-lowered or hidden away entirely, depending on individual taste.

ABOVE *In this guest room a roller blind based on a spring mechanism has been combined with a muslin swag to provide privacy at night. The dark green fabric of the blind also keeps out the morning light.*

LEFT AND RIGHT *This typical Swedish blind is constructed by the traditional leather thong and glass ring method. The leather is attached to the wooden batten at the top of the blind and holds in place two glass rings. The string used to raise and lower the blind is threaded through these rings. A thin wooden batten held in a pocket at the bottom of the fabric keeps the lower edge straight.*

A TRADITIONAL BLIND

*This traditional form of blind is seen in windows all over Sweden, either hung on its own
or with a muslin swag. Woven checked linen, left unlined to let in a maximum amount of light,
is an attractive and appropriate choice of material as the blind rolls upwards and inwards,
revealing both sides of the fabric.*

MATERIALS AND EQUIPMENT

Fabric
25mm/1in x 12mm/½in
wooden batten the width
of the blind
12mm/½in diameter wooden
dowel the width of the blind
Two glass, brass or
plastic rings
Two 25mm/1in screws
Two 75mm/3in x 6mm/¼in
strips of leather
Roll of blind string
Window cleat

or

Swedish blind kit

MEASURING AND SEWING THE FABRIC

1 Cut your fabric so that it
about 10cm/4in wider and
about 15cm/6in longer than
the inner edge of your window
frame. This is to allow for the
hems and a small overlap
between the blind and the
window frame.

2 Create the side hems by
folding the two long edges in
twice by 12mm/½in. Iron in
folds and sew down the hem
using a machine. If using a
checked fabric, make sure the
checks align, as light will show
through the edges of the blind.

3 Turn down the top 12mm/
½in of the blind, iron and sew
down. Turn down a further
30mm/1¼in to make a pocket
for the batten and sew down.
Turn up the bottom 12mm/
½in of the blind, iron and sew
down. Turn up a further
25mm/1in to make a pocket for
the dowelling, and sew down.

MAKING THE BLIND

4 Insert a wooden batten the
width of the blind in the top
pocket. Place the two pieces of
thonging, folded in half with a
glass ring in each fold, about
15cm/6in from either side.
Use a bradawl to make a hole
so the fabric does not twist,
then drill through the leather
loops and wooden batten and
insert the 25mm/1in screws.
You will need to string the
blind before you finally
position it at the window,

as the cord is suspended from
the two screws attached to the
window frame. Insert the
wooden dowel in the bottom
pocket. Following the cording
diagram above, string the
blind. Do not forget to leave a

long loop at the front so that
the blind can be raised and
lowered. Drill two holes in
the window frame and screw
the blind in position. Screw
the cleat to the side of the
window frame and wrap the
long loop of cord around it to
hold the blind in the desired
position.

ACCESSORIES

TRADITIONAL SWEDISH STYLE employs a minimum of accessories, but a great deal of thought is given to their selection and positioning. Although craftsmanship is highly valued, most pieces are chosen for their usefulness as well as for their visual appeal. Empty space is generally not considered an embarrassment, and surfaces are not cluttered with a muddle of objects. A side table or chest of drawers may be crowned by no more than a simple bowl or a pair of candlesticks. An exquisitely laid table may be adorned with a single white flower in a glass rather than a large vase of multicoloured blooms. Woven rag rugs and runners in checks or random stripes bring a touch of colour to bleached wooden floors and are usually preferred to fitted carpets.

The Swedes love to invite guests to dine and enjoy the chance to indulge their sense of occasion. Table settings are important: they relish the gleam of silver cutlery and candlesticks, the feel of crisp starched

The vast chimney breast in the kitchen of this manor house near Stockholm once housed the cooking stove. It has now been converted to provide an original display area for a collection of antique kitchen copper. Below an elegant gold and white lamp, the table is set for a family lunch. Antique blue and white Meissen china, crystal glasses, polished silver and a single brass candlestick gleam against the dark wood of an old rustic-style table. Its set of matching chairs have been given cushions in a traditional blue and grey check. A single accent of bright colour is provided by the salmon-pink pelargonium in its copper container.

linen and the sparkle of crystal glasses and chandeliers. Much of their tableware is characterized by elegance and formality and it is true to say that even family meals in Sweden are served from serving dishes, rather than straight from the pan in which the food is cooked. Elaborate serving platters, covered soup and vegetable dishes, coffee sets that include dainty side plates, cream jugs and sugar bowls are all quite at home in a Gustavian-style setting.

Tableware

By choosing one's accessories carefully, it is easy – and can be inexpensive – to create the illusion of dining in an eighteenth-century Swedish manor house, whether you live in an apartment in Washington or Paris, or in a village in the Cotswolds. Scouring the antique shops can turn up some truly authentic-looking glass, china, cutlery and linen, usually at a price. Alternatively, there are excellent reproduction pieces to be had, or modern designs that are clearly inspired by eighteenth-century Neoclassicism. Up until the mid eighteenth century the cost of silver meant that most Swedes used its imitation, pewter, for the table. Nowadays, however, silverware is highly valued. If you can afford it, silver cutlery in classic styles, either original or reproduction, will add the finishing touch to a Gustavian table, but pewter in the same style looks charming if kept well polished.

Until the late 1700s, glazed, porous earthenware, or faience, was used for eating and serving dishes by most people. Then the import of vast quantities of

porcelain from China by the Swedish East India Company had its impact on Swedish taste. They greatly admired the qualities of refinement and restraint that they found in these wares, and soon discovered that they were well suited to their own interiors. The blue and white designs of Chinese porcelain became, and have remained, particularly popular. Initially there was strong resistance to the idea of Swedish-made porcelain. People wanting porcelain dinner and tea services ordered them directly from China, sending out a drawing of the required pattern via the traders of the Swedish East India Company. Eventually, however, a homegrown industry evolved. The factories at Rörstrand (founded 1726) and Marieberg (founded 1758, but later bought up by Rörstrand), were originally producers of faience, but their porcelain finally found a market, and some of the blue and white patterns that are most popular today, and most closely identified with Scandinavia, have their origins in Rörstrand designs.

As well as the Chinese-inspired blue and white tableware, plain white bone china or white decorated with a simple gold edge or other classical gold design is perfectly acceptable for the Gustavian look. Pale blue, pale yellow or grey are other possible base colours, while simple decorations can include small central flower motifs, delicate lined rims or dainty floral swags. Many modern tableware designs incorporate similar motifs; otherwise you might find suitable examples in antique shops. You may also find early twentieth-century tableware in the Neoclassical revivalist style that would pass for Gustavian pieces.

GLASS

Before the eighteenth century, glass was very expensive in Sweden, and its use was restricted to the aristocracy. Although the Kungsholm factory that provided the glass pendants for the chandeliers at Gripsholm was founded in 1676, the two firms of Kosta and Orrefors, now well-known for the quality of their drinking glasses, were not established until 1742 and 1898 respectively. Much modern Swedish glass is coloured or has touches of colour on a stem or on a handle, but the Gustavian look demands colourless glass in simple shapes. In the eighteenth century, when glass was handblown, it had a chunky look and drinking glasses with twisted stems or with a 'teardrop' in the stem were common styles. Nowadays such patterns are copied by modern glassworks, but often in the finer crystal that twentieth-century manufacturing techniques can produce. For the Gustavian look the glass should either be plain, or etched with classical swags, posies or monograms.

A formally laid Swedish dinner table will include drinking glasses in many sizes. First there will be a small *snaps* (schnapps) glass, for *snaps* has long been part of Swedish drinking habits. Working men used to take it as part-payment of their day's wages, as employers believed that they needed extra fortification in the extreme cold. Now it is usually drunk with a herring or gravad laks hors d'oeuvre. There will also be two wine glasses, one for red and one for white wine, as well as a water goblet and sometimes a glass for a sweet dessert wine. For everyday meals, beer, again in a special glass, and milk are usually preferred to wine.

ABOVE *This painted cupboard houses a family collection of crystal glassware and a range of china from gilded and painted procelain to traditional blue and white.*

LEFT *Elegant table accessories are a prerequisite in Swedish homes. Antique white china is sometimes decorated with gold, with a few painted sprigs of pink flowers or with Chinese blue and white designs. Glasses are often etched with delicate swags or monograms. Even in the most modest household, there will be table linen, often embroidered and passed down through the family for generations.*

Embroidery

Times of hardship have made the Swedes extremely resourceful in various ways, but especially in their use of decorative textiles. When their purses could not run to the expense of rich tapestries on the walls, they hung painted linen canvas instead. Material was often re-used. There are examples of seventeenth-century quilted bedcovers in peasant homes that were made from pieces of women's skirts, doubtless cut up and resewn when they became worn or when fashions changed. Similarly, *kurbits* painting did not have to be done at great cost on a large expanse of wall. It could be executed simply on whatever came to hand – offcuts of wood, flour sacks or tablecloths. There is even an example of a *kurbits* painting on cloth taken from a man's shirt on which the seams of the sleeves are visible at the sides of the picture.

After the death of Gustav III, European – and especially French – influence over Swedish interior design became so overwhelming that the Swedes almost lost sight of their own excellence in this field. However, mid nineteenth-century romanticism and later the Arts and Crafts movement helped to reawaken interest in the use of native Swedish materials and traditional crafts such as weaving and embroidery. Karin, the wife of Carl Larsson, was a weaver. One of her contributions to the now-famous house at Lilla Hyttnäs was a beautiful collection of traditional woven and embroidered bedspreads, bedhangings, tablecloths, rag rugs and cotton runners. These blended well with the pared-down simplicity and cool elegance of the Gustavian elements

ABOVE *A worn and faded cross-stitched sampler has been made into a pretty cushion. Worked on unbleached linen, the pinky red of the thread has always been a popular colour in Sweden. The name Alice Nordin, which can just be made out below the alphabets, presumably identifies the embroiderer.*

RIGHT *This selection shows some of the vast range of decorative household linen common in Sweden to this day. Monograms on towels, table and bed linen vary from naive outlined letters, like the simple W surmounted by two birds, to splendid ornate designs worked above a band of mixed woven and embroidered decoration. Several techniques have been used to beautify a bedhanging. Together with an exuberant floral design in the peasant tradition, there is a crocheted edge and a striped fringe.*

of the home – the painted furniture, plain white curtains and the checked and striped upholstery fabrics.

A strong tradition of embroidery was evident at all levels of society. In richer households, monograms were used as a way of identifying items of linen, for they were expensive and had to be accounted for. Similarly in peasant homes, when a woman married she was expected to bring all the towels and bedlinen with her as part of her dowry, and she and other female members of her family would embroider it to look as beautiful as possible. Although the craft is dying out now, embroidered or monogrammed linen used to be passed down through families for generations.

Taking as their raw material the natural, unbleached linen that was universally available, peasant women transformed it into every conceivable type of practical yet decorative item for the home. They wove rugs and bedhangings. They embroidered using the colours that are still popular today – yellows, pinks, reds and greens. Red was especially popular as it symbolized love and fertility. They used cross-stitch and satin-stitch to make stylized flowers, animal and human figures, often in borders edging a piece of linen. They used thread-counting techniques and drawn-threadwork and added lace and crochet.

Peasant women also made decorative cloths for hanging over cupboards and clocks. Cushion covers took a variety of forms, including bridal cushions embroidered with the initials of the bride and groom, or long cushions made to fit unupholstered benches around the edge of the room. They spent hours decorating

bed textiles, for these were the most important part of a woman's dowry. Hangings were made simply to drape over a quilted bedcover so that their decorated hems faced the viewer. Pillowslips were designed to be placed with one unadorned short edge against the wall and the other short, elaborately embroidered edge, facing into the room. In the days when wooden homes were built with high, open ceilings, these would be decked on festive occasions. The sloping ceilings and the walls would be covered with woven, embroidered or painted hangings, all usually made of linen. This custom died out when flat ceilings were installed and walls were papered or painted.

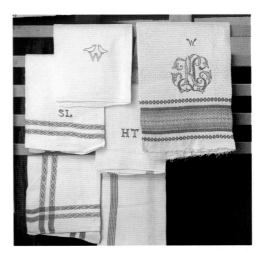

Table linen provided another excuse for decoration and has remained an important part of entertaining. If a white linen cloth covering an entire table could not be afforded, there would be small mats marking out the places of the most distinguished people present. In more wealthy homes, a white linen or damask cloth always covered the table, providing a source of reflected light in a room that was lit only by candles.

If you want to copy the Swedish look, it is possible to find beautiful old table or bed linen in shops specializing in antique textiles. You may be lucky enough to come across a tablecloth with a matching set of napkins – often as many as twelve – although in the eighteenth century napkins were not so common. Linen, plain or with a simple diaper pattern, or in the very expensive linen damask form, is best. It can be embellished with some white embroidery or white lace. A disadvantage of pure linen is that it is best to have it professionally laundered.

A CROSS-STITCH MOTIF FOR LINEN

Although most table linen is monogrammed with the owner's initials, a slightly less personal motif makes an interesting variation. Flowers, birds and urns are all widely used, but the royal crown is a typically Swedish motif. Here it has been cross-stitched onto ready-made linen napkins, which would make a delightful gift.

MATERIALS AND EQUIPMENT

Finely woven linen
napkins with an
even weave
Pins
Embroidery needle
Stranded embroidery
cotton

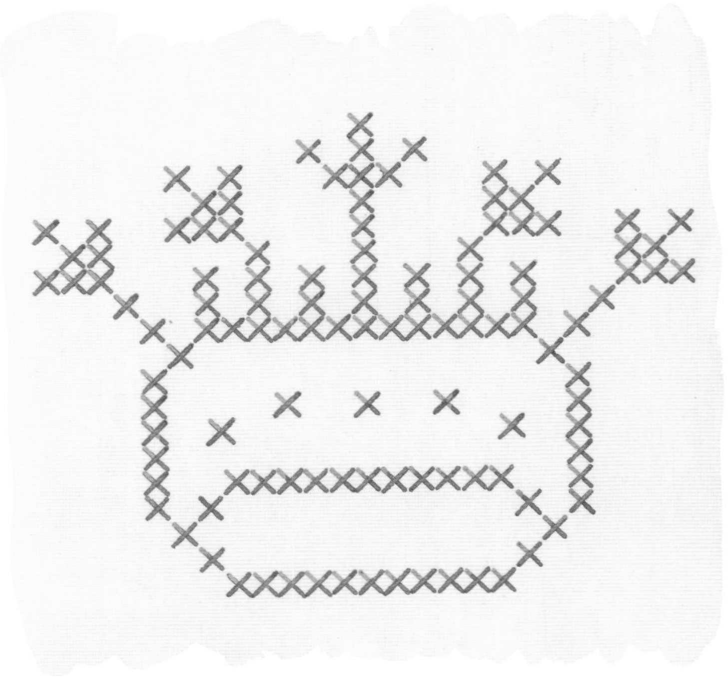

POSITIONING THE CROWN

1 To mark where the crown is to go on a napkin, fold it the way you would for a place setting and mark the centre with a pin. The one shown here is placed on the bottom right-hand corner 75mm/ 3in from the bottom of the napkin and 50mm/2in from the right edge. The crown measures 30mm/1¼in wide by 25mm/1in high. The napkin measures 44cm/17½in square.

CROSS STITCH TECHNIQUE

2 Refer to the chart above. For a long row of cross stitch it is best to work an entire row of diagonals in one direction and then double back to complete the crosses with a further row of diagonals **(top)**. For isolated stitches complete each stitch as you go along **(bottom)**.

The cross stitch shown here is worked over two threads of the linen, but on a finer weave you can embroider over three threads. When joining in new strands of cotton, do not knot the ends but pass them under worked stitches on the back.

SEWING THE CROWN

3 Thread the needle with three strands of embroidery cotton and begin working the motif where the pin is. This will be the bottom centre of the crown, so you need to count the stitches out from either side. Leaving a loose end at the back of the work, start embroidering the rows from bottom to top, catching the loose end into the work as you go along. When the napkin is finished press lightly on the wrong side under a damp cloth.

Rugs

Woven rugs and runners have traditionally offered another way of decorating the home without vast expense, and could be found even in sophisticated eighteenth-century manor houses. Most Swedish woven rugs are made either entirely of linen or cotton, or from a thick warp thread interwoven with narrow lengths of rag. The rags are usually cut from worn-out clothing or oddments left over from dress-making. Practical and hardwearing, both kinds of rug may be used as narrow runners at the foot of a bed, in front of a sofa, in a hallway, underneath a table or in the distinctive Swedish way as strips running around the edges of a room and folded into mitres at the corners.

Although rag rugs in random colours and patterns are widely available, for the Gustavian look you should confine your choice to the traditional colours of the Gustavian palette, either in a random pattern or in one of the many striped or chequered designs. A red, grey and cream striped rag rug, for example, could look very effective with a grey-painted chair upholstered in red and cream gingham.

LEFT *In this hallway, with its pair of decorative wooden benches, the only pattern is provided by a woven linen rug in bold green and white check.*

RIGHT *Each of these rugs was specially woven to match the decor in four rooms of a guesthouse. Stripes, checks and a subtle diamond pattern in traditional colours mix well with the printed and woven patterns of the furnishing fabric. It is this sort of attention to detail that sets the Swedish style apart.*

Lighting

In a country that is in the dark for so much of the year, light is crucial. Before the advent of electricity, Swedes in every kind of home made imaginative use of reflecting surfaces, such as glass, crystal and even polished metal, to increase the light produced by candles. Similar effects can be achieved without a great deal of expense today and can be used either alone or with subdued electric lighting.

CANDLESTICKS AND CHANDELIERS

The Swedes use candles a great deal in their homes, often lighting them as dusk falls to welcome members of the family back from work or school. To mark the shortest days of the year and to remind people that more daylight is on its way, the feast of St Lucia is still widely celebrated on 13 December, ushered in by a girl dressed in a long white robe, who wears a crown of white candles.

In Gustavian times, of course, candles would have been the main source of artificial light, although many homes would have kept an oil lamp burning by the hearth. Among the simplest of these was the *cruisie*, a shallow lipped bowl containing oil, into which a wick was laid. In the wealthiest houses candles were used in sparkling crystal chandeliers or in solid silver candlesticks or candelabra. These look wonderful on a table with a white cloth, or on a painted side table, as do crystal candlesticks, but less expensive and equally acceptable substitutes are candlesticks of brass or pewter, or even china or wood. If you cannot afford genuine antique candlesticks, there are many modern reproduction designs in all

materials. Be sure to use only white candles for the authentic look of the eighteenth century.

Crystal has always been popular in Sweden, because it reflects light both day and night. Gripsholm was well furnished with crystal chandeliers in myriad styles, many of them supplied in the mid 1700s with glass pendants from the Kungsholm glassworks. Hanging low over a dining table, crystal chandeliers – even modern electrified versions – give out a warm, intimate light. If you cannot find or cannot afford genuine old chandeliers, good reproductions are available, but do try to find those in which the crystal pendants are held together with fine brass wires, not attached to the heavy gilded bands that are sometimes seen today.

A less costly, but equally authentic alternative is a ceiling lantern of glass panels held together by a decorated metal framework. Fitted with candles in metal holders, such lanterns were designed to hang in the centre of the room.

SCONCES

To provide light from the walls as well as from the ceiling, candles were also used in wall sconces of various shapes and sizes. The beauty of the sconce was that, like the crystal chandelier, it served to magnify the light of the candle or pair of candles. With a mirror-glass backing – the mirror was often bevelled or etched to create more surfaces and edges off which the light could bounce – a sconce can add real eighteenth-century elegance to a room. In some Swedish examples the backing was made of gilded wood or of faience. The glistening gilt or the white surface of the faience were almost as reflective as mirror-glass. A polished metal backing, while slightly less efficient, added a warm glow to the candle-light.

Old examples are hard to find, but there are many lovely reproduction sconces available. Look for mirrored versions with discreet gilt or wooden frames, perhaps topped with a carved bow or plume. Over-bright gilding on a new piece can be rubbed back with fine sandpaper to give it a more authentic aged look, while a carved wooden frame can be 'Gustavianized' with a marbled finish or with a coat of pearl-grey paint, perhaps antiqued with a little yellow ochre. If you are looking for reproduction pieces, choose the simplest possible styles, decorated with classically inspired motifs – wreaths, urns, quivers of arrows, scallop shells, and so on.

Mirrors themselves were another feature of Gustavian interiors that are easy to introduce in your own home. Again, they were much prized for adding light to a room, although mirror-glass was heavily taxed and until the nineteenth century could not be made in big pieces. A practical solution was to make larger mirrors from several pieces of glass joined together. Pier glasses were especially popular in Sweden in the late eighteenth century and look very elegant if you happen to have a pair of windows to flank one. A painted dropleaf table in front of the glass will complete the effect beautifully. As with sconces, choose mirror frames that have an uncluttered, no-frills look. Some judicious distressing of an over-bright frame will make it look more like an original.

ABOVE *Panelled walls, delicate taffeta curtains and a candle-lit chandelier all contribute to the Swedish feeling achieved in this London bedroom. A gold-leafed mirror propped against the wall adds light and space to a corner of the room.*

LEFT *Three examples of antique crystal chandeliers, both electrified and candle-lit, that would suit the finest Swedish room.*

OVERLEAF *Mirrors and sconces come in many guises and sizes, though most incorporate a gilded area of some kind to help reflect the light of the candles.*

Carefully placed accessories have an important part to play in the Swedish interior. Aim for quality rather than quantity. An unusually shaped tôle (painted metal) tea caddy, a silk embroidered picture, etched or cut glass and delicately gilded objects with a Neo-classical flavour, would all add authentic finishing touches to an elegant decorative scheme.

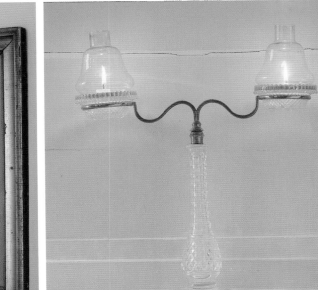

Sources

UNITED KINGDOM

The Blue Door
77 Church Road
Barnes, London SW13 9HH
0181 748 9785
*Furniture, fabrics, blind fittings,
antiques, accessories, decorating service*

Manuel Canovas
2 North Terrace
London SW3 2BA
0171 225 2298
Checked and striped fabrics

The Ceramic Stove Company
4 Earl Street
Oxford OX2 0JA
01865 245 077
Reproduction ceramic stoves

Farrow and Ball
35 Uddens Trading Estate
Wimborne
Dorset BH21 7NL
01202 876 141
Manufacturers of traditional paints

Pierre Frey
253 Fulham Road
London SW3 6HY
0171 376 5599
Checked and striped fabrics

IKEA
*Swedish furniture, fabrics and
accessories. Reproduction Gustavian
furniture collection available only at
stores marked **

IKEA Birmingham
Park Lane
Wednesbury
West Midlands WS10 9SF
0121 526 5232

IKEA Brent Park*
2 Drury Way
North Circular Road
London NW10 0TH
0181 208 5600

IKEA Croydon*
Valley Park
Purley Way
Croydon CR0 4UZ
0181 208 5601

IKEA Gateshead
Metro Park West
Gateshead
Tyne and Wear
NE11 9XS
0191 461 0202

IKEA Leeds
Holden Ing Way
Birstall
Batley WF17 9AE
01924 423 296

IKEA Thurrock Lakeside
Heron Way
West Thurrock
Grays RM20 3WJ
01375 360 738

IKEA Warrington
Gemini Retail Park
910 Europa Boulevard
Warrington WA5 5TY
01925 655 889

Jorgen Antiques
40 Lower Richmond Road
London SW15 1JP
0181 789 7329
*High quality antiques and
accessories from all over
Scandinavia*

Kingshill Designs
Kitchener Works
Kitchener Road
High Wycombe
Bucks HP11 2SH
01494 463 910
*Modern collection of Swedish
furniture*

Ian Mankin (Natural Fabrics)
Ltd
109 Regents Park Road
Primrose Hill
London NW1 8UR
0171 722 0997
*Good range of checked and striped
fabrics*

Nobilis Fontan
1-2 Cedar Studios
45 Glebe Place
London SW3 5JE
0171 351 7878
*Reproduction Gustavian furniture,
traditional fabrics and wallpapers
(trade only)*

Nordic Style at Moussie
109 Walton Street
London SW3 2PH
0171 581 8674
Reproduction furniture, accessories

Harriet Ann Sleigh Beds
Standen Farm
Smarden Road
Biddenden
Nr. Ashford
Kent TN27 8JT
01580 291 220
Scandinavian antique beds

SWEDEN

Solgården
Neglingevägen 33
13334 Saltsjöbaden
Sweden
08 717 57 00
*Reproduction furniture, accessories,
decorating service*

PersiennGruppen
Karlavägen 66
Stockholm
08 661 44 00
*Suppliers of Swedish blind kits by
mail order*

USA

IKEA
496 West Germanstown Pike
Plymouth Meeting, PA 19462
(610) 834 0180 for an IKEA
near you
*Wide range of inexpensive, good
quality furniture you assemble
yourself*

CALIFORNIA

Gustavus af Kingsberg
1520 Draper Street
Kingsberg, CA 93631
(209) 897 1657
*Imported reproductions of
Neoclassical, Gustavian style
furniture*

Nordiska Butik
771 Monterey Boulevard
San Franscisco, CA 94127
(415) 239 8107
*Gifts, linens and accessories
imported from Sweden*

Svensk Butik
1465 Draper Street
Kingsberg, CA 93631
(209) 897 5119
Large array of Swedish textiles and fabrics as well as accessories and imported country pine furniture

CONNECTICUT
Country Swedish
35 Post Road West
Westport, CT 06880
(203) 222 8212
Classic Swedish fabrics and reproductions of traditional wallpapers and 18th- and 19th-century Gustavian furniture

FLORIDA
Copenhagen Imports
7211 South Tamiami Trail
Sarasota, FL 34231
(813) 923 2560
Importer of contemporary Scandinavian furniture

Lars Bolander Limited
375 South County Road
Palm Beach, FL 33480
(407) 832 2121
Swedish antiques and reproductions

ILLINOIS
Barbara A. Johnson Antiques
7801 East State Street
Rockford, IL 61125
(815) 397 6699
Swedish antiques. A wide variety of waxed pine and painted pieces

IOWA
Harley Refsal
619 North Street
Decorah, IA 52101
(319) 382 9383
Scandinavian-style basswood figure carvings. By appointment only

MARYLAND
Scan Contemporary Furniture
13701 Georgia Avenue
Silver Spring, MD 20906
(301) 942 0600
Scandinavian country furniture in a variety of woods

MASSACHUSETTS
Ingrid Interiors
177 Tilden Road
Scituate, MA 02066
(617) 545 5237
Designer Ingrid Goulston offers a wide selection of country Swedish fabrics and wallpaper and reproduction furniture

MINNESOTA
Blondell Antiques
1406 Second Street SW
Rochester, MN 55902
(507) 282 1872
High quality, painted Swedish classic country furniture and accessories dating from the late 17th to the early 19th century. The furniture is imported or purchased from Scandinavian immigrants

Country Collection Antiques
213 East First Avenue
Shakopee, MN 55379
(612) 445 1500
Scandinavian furniture, including bench beds, cupboards, tables, textiles and ironware, which is imported or purchased from immigrants

International Design Center
100 Second Avenue North
Minneapolis, MN 55401
(612) 341 3441
Wide selection of high quality, contemporary Scandinavian furniture

The Swedish Timber House
7687 Interlachen Road
Nisswa, MN 56468
(218) 963 7897
Gift store offering Scandinavian handicrafts and handwoven textiles

NEW YORK
ABC Carpet and Home
888 Broadway
New York, NY 10003
(212) 473 3000
Wide selection of Scandinavian pine furniture

Arne V. Schlesch
158 East 64th Street
New York, NY 10021
(212) 838 3923
Dealer in fine quality, 18th-century Scandinavian antiques

Eileen Lane Antiques
150 Thompson Street
New York, NY 10012
(212) 475 2988
Swedish furniture of the 19th and 20th centuries, especially Biedermeier and Art Deco styles

Evergreen Antiques Inc.
1249 Third Avenue
New York, NY 10021
(212) 744 5664
Primarily Scandinavian country pine furniture

Lars Bolander Limited
5 Toilsome Lane
East Hampton, NY 11937
(516) 329 3400
Swedish antiques and reproductions

Macy's Corner Shop Antique Galleries
151 West 34th Street, 9th Floor
New York, NY 10001
(212) 494 4049
Scandinavian antique and reproduction furniture ranging from Biedermeier to country pine

Valley House Antiques
By appointment
(516) 671 2847
Swedish furniture and accessories of the 18th and 19th centuries, especially Biedermeier

Victor Antiques, Ltd.
223 East 60th Street
New York, NY 10022
(212) 752 4100
Swedish Biedermeier furniture and accessories

TEXAS
Wooden Spoon
1617 Avenue K
Plano, TX
(214) 424 6867
Accessories and textiles imported from Sweden

VIRGINIA
Skandina Inc.
Box 2053
8 South Madison Street
Middleburg, VA 20118
(540) 687 3730
A wide offering of Scandinavian furniture, gifts and accessories

WISCONSIN
Suzanne Jameson Kramer Country Gallery Antiques
136 150th Street
River Falls, WI 54022
(715) 425 7107
Scandinavian country pine and birch furniture from the 18th to the early 20th centuries. Open by appointment only

Index

BIBLIOGRAPHY

Alderton, Mary Blue Guide to Sweden *A. & C. Black/Norton, 1995*

Barwick, JoAnn Scandinavian Country *Thames and Hudson/Clarkson Potter, 1991*

Bowman, Monica, ed. Design in Sweden *Elsevier, 1985*

Brooklyn Museum, The Carl Larsson *Holt, Rinehart, and Winston, 1983*

de Dampierre, Florence The Best of Painted Furniture *Rizzoli, 1987*

Derry, T.K. A History of Scandinavia *George Allen and Unwin, 1979*

Drayton, Louise, and Jane Thomson The Stencil Book *Dorling Kindersley, 1994*

Edenheim, Ralph Skansen: Traditional Swedish Style *Scala Books, 1995*

Franck, Harry Alverson A Scandinavian Summer *Century Company, 1930*

Gaynor, Elizabeth Scandinavian Living Design *Thames and Hudson/ Stewart, Tabori and Chang, 1987*

Groth, Håkan Neoclassicism in the North: Swedish Furniture and Interiors 1770-1850 *Thames and Hudson/Rizzoli, 1990*

Hallendorff, Carl, and Adolf Schuck History of Sweden *C.E. Fritze, 1929*

Hultin, Olof, ed. Architecture in Sweden *Arkitectur Forlag AB, 1983*

Innes, Jocasta Scandinavian Painted Furniture *Cassell/Random House, 1990*

Innes, Jocasta Scandinavian Painted Decor *Cassell, 1992*

Innes, Jocasta The New Decorator's Handbook *HarperCollins, 1995*

Larsson, Carl Our Home *Methuen Children's Books, 1976*

McCloud, Kevin Decorative Style *Simon and Schuster, 1990*

Meehan, Patricia Stencil Sourcebook: Over 200 New Designs *North Light Books, 1994*

Miller, Judith and Martin Country Style *Mitchell Beazley, 1990*

di Niscemi, Maita Manor Houses and Castles of Sweden *Scala Books, 1988*

Plath, Iona The Decorative Arts of Sweden *Dover, 1965*

af Segerstad, Ulf Hard Carl Larsson's Home *Addison-Wesley, 1978*

Scobbie, Irene Sweden *Scarecrow Press, 1972*

Sjöberg, Lars and Ursula The Swedish Room *Frances Lincoln/Pantheon, 1994*

Sloan, Annie The Practical Guide to Decorative Antique Effects *Collins and Brown, 1995*

Söderburg, Bengt G. Manor Houses and Royal Castles in Sweden *Malmö, 1975*

Taylor, Doreen, ed. Insight Guides: Sweden, *A.P.A. Publications, 1990*

Thornton, Peter Authentic Decor: The Domestic Interior 1620-1920 *Weidenfeld and Nicolson/Viking, 1984*

von Heidenstrum, Oscar Gustaf Swedish Life in Town and Country *Putnams, 1904*

Wiles, Richard Quick and Easy Painted Furniture *Ward Lock, 1995*

AUTHOR'S ACKNOWLEDGMENTS

This book has been a pleasure to work on from beginning to end, and this is due in large part to the people who have been instrumental in its making. Special thanks are due to Anna Lallerstedt Thomas, who accompanied me on my first memorable and happy trip to Sweden, and gave me the opportunity to experience the true hospitality of the Swedish people. While taking the photographs in Sweden we encountered nothing but kindness and help from Merrill Stendbeck, Patty Hansel, Lillemor and Hans Jakobsson, Fred and Catarina Wennerholm, Göran and Catharina Groth, Margareta Biörck, Eva Biörck-Belfrage, Martine Colliander, Johan and Irene Seth, Marita Wikander at Skansen, Lars and Ulrika Olsson, Hasse Jordan and Annika Gunnarsson also at Skansen, to name but a few – *tack så mycket*. In England, Catharina Mannerfelt has been instrumental in helping with this book; her shop The Blue Door in Barnes is a perfect little parcel of all that is Sweden. She has opened her doors to us and allowed us to photograph her wonderful antiques and reproductions. Annie Beck and Lena Spindler-Bock helped endlessly and patiently while I raided the shop of their best stock.

Thank you to Christopher Drake for the beautiful photographs and to Anne Wilson and Caroline Bugler at Frances Lincoln. Tabby Riley painted many of the original projects with her usual professionalism and sensitivity; many thanks. Thanks go also to Vanessa Berridge and Hilary Mandelburg for all their help with the text, and to Peter Thornton who kindly cast his most learned eye over the book. Carolyn Brunton, my agent, a truly stalwart lady, who sadly will not see this book published, is and will always be missed.

And finally to the home team. These books require some time spent away from home, husbands and children, and I was lucky enough to have a great support system: my large and close family, Janey Joicey-Cecil, Catherine Coombes, Chris, Eddie and Jo Turner.

PUBLISHERS' ACKNOWLEDGMENTS

The publishers are grateful to Christine O'Brien, Brigitta Wäng-Folan, Paula Örnsjö and Ruth Carim for their editorial assistance and Susanne Haines and Amanda Patton for their artwork.

Project Editor Caroline Bugler
Assistant Editor James Bennett
Designer Anne Wilson
Picture Editor Anne Fraser
Production Kim van Woerkom
Index Helen Baz
Editorial Director Erica Hunningher
Art Director Caroline Hillier